WE MADE URANIUM!

WE MADE URANIUM!

AND OTHER TRUE STORIES FROM THE UNIVERSITY OF CHICAGO'S EXTRAORDINARY SCAVENGER HUNT

EDITED BY **LEILA SALES**

THE UNIVERSITY OF CHICAGO PRESS
CHICAGO AND LONDON

The University of Chicago Press, Chicago 60637
The University of Chicago Press, Ltd., London
© 2019 by Leila Sales
All rights reserved. No part of this book may be used or reproduced in
any manner whatsoever without written permission, except in the case
of brief quotations in critical articles and reviews. For more information,
contact the University of Chicago Press, 1427 E. 60th St., Chicago, IL 60637.
Published 2019
Printed in the United States of America

28 27 26 25 24 23 22 21 20 19   1 2 3 4 5

ISBN-13: 978-0-226-57184-3   (paper)
ISBN-13:978- 0-226-57198-0   (e-book)
DOI: https://doi.org/10.7208/chicago/9780226571980.001.0001

LIBRARY OF CONGRESS CATALOGING-IN-PUBLICATION DATA

Names: Sales, Leila, editor.
Title: We made uranium! : and other true stories from the University of
    Chicago's extraordinary Scavenger Hunt / edited by Leila Sales.
Description: Chicago ; London : The University of Chicago Press, 2019.
Identifiers: LCCN 2018054723 | ISBN 9780226571706 (cloth : alk. paper)
    ISBN 9780226571843 (pbk. : alk. paper) | ISBN 9780226571980 (e-book)
Subjects: LCSH: University of Chicago—Undergraduates. | College stu-
    dents—Illinois—Chicago—Social life and customs. | Undergraduates—Il-
    linois—Chicago—Social life and customs. | Treasure hunt (Game)—Illi-
    nois—Chicago. | Chicago (Ill.)—Social life and customs.
Classification: LCC LD936.W46 2019 | DDC 378.1/980977311—dc23
LC record available at https://lccn.loc.gov/2018054723

♾ This paper meets the requirements of ANSI/NISO Z39.48–1992
(Permanence of Paper).

This book is dedicated to all the Scavvies and Judges who make dreams come true.

CONTENTS

INTRODUCTION

In the spring of 1987, on the campus of the prestigious University of Chicago, a group of students held a scavenger hunt. It was, generally speaking, a normal scavenger hunt. The list asked for some standard items (e.g., item 39: "A four-leaf clover," or item 106: "A pinecone"); some harder-to-find items, especially since this was in the days before the internet (e.g., item 165: "A ball and chain," or item 142: "A completed Sunday *New York Times* crossword puzzle"); and a few impossible but humorous items (e.g., item 6: "Bruce Willis (my roomie wants him, she will pay a bonus for him)").

Some of the items were kind of geeky in their wording (e.g., item 7: "An item that contains Sodium Monourophosphate"— solution: toothpaste), but that wasn't a surprise. This was, after all, the University of Chicago, which prides itself on being a welcoming home for nerds, with eighty-nine Nobel laureates to its name, a school where on a Friday night you'll find a more impressive scene at the library than at a frat house. According to the T-shirts, the U of C is "where fun comes to die," and this scavenger hunt was an attempt to revive some fun in a spring quarter that otherwise felt much too long, cold, and academically challenging.

But that wasn't where the scavenger hunt stopped. Not even close.

Over the past three decades, the University of Chicago scavenger hunt—now called Scav Hunt—has grown and morphed into one of the most bizarre, outrageous annual traditions at any university. Disregard anything you might

remember from childhood birthday party activities, and forget about four-leaf clovers and pinecones. Scav Hunt is now a
four-day extravaganza of barely controlled chaos. Hundreds
of students and alumni compete to fulfill 300-plus items,
all of which can be achieved within a 1,000-mile radius of
campus. And simply finding things is only a small part of it.
Many items must be invented, built, or performed.

Over the years, competitors have shown that there's very
little they won't do for Scav. For Scav, people have gotten married, spent four days handcuffed together, gotten permanent
tattoos, eaten their own umbilical cords, taken planes without
knowing where they were going or why, dragged elephants on
to the university campus, been circumcised, built a working
nuclear reactor . . . the list goes on. Participants have poured
their literal blood, sweat, tears, and other bodily fluids into
Scav. (And also bodily solids, as per item 156 of the 2009 Hunt:
"Take a running shit.") If Scavvies have never killed for points,
it's only because the Judges haven't asked them to.

At this point you might be asking *why*. Why would these
presumably intelligent young adults, students at one of the
top-ranked colleges in the world, devote their brainpower
and resources to building a human-sized game of Mouse
Trap or a piano that plays alcoholic beverages? Surely there
must be a huge prize to make all this effort worth it?

No. There's not. The winning team may get a couple hundred bucks, but I can't swear to that, and even if they do, it just
goes straight into funding the team's Scav efforts for the next
year. I competed as a Scavvie for three years before becoming
a Judge, and my team won one or maybe two of those years,
and all I remember getting was some Häagen-Dazs and a T-
shirt that I still sometimes wear to the gym. The question of
whether your team wins is generally so unimportant that *I
can't even remember* if mine did it once or twice.

The point of Scav is not to win a big prize, and to some

extent it's not about winning at all. *The point of Scav is to do cool shit.* That's it. And this is a book about some of the cool shit that Scavvies have done.

There is a story behind every item on the List. You just can't eat your own umbilical cord without getting a story to tell about it. And this book is a collection of some of these stories, spread over the course of many years of the Hunt, written by Scavvies themselves. This is not a complete history, but rather individuals' unique and unforgettable experiences from the past thirty years of Scav Hunt.

THE FOUR DAYS

The essays that follow will make a bit more sense if you have a general understanding of the structure of the Hunt. This structure has shifted and developed over the years, but it is always roughly as follows.

There is a panel of Judges who spend the school year creating the List. The Judgeship is made up of about a dozen current students, who often have previous experience competing in Scav Hunt, as well as many alumni Judges who maintain their emeritus status. The Judges brainstorm and workshop items, debate, vote, come up with wording and pointing, and ultimately wind up with around 300 items that constitute the List.

The Judges assign a maximum point score to each item, loosely tied to how challenging the item would be to complete. A simple "go find it" item, trivia item, or minor "be clever" item might be worth a couple points (for example, item 39 of the 2000 Hunt, "A box of Honey Nut Beerios," was worth a maximum of 7 points). Each list will also have perhaps two or three items called "showcase items" that are pointed in the hundreds, usually large and complicated construction items. (For example, item 18 of the 2008 Hunt,

"A parade balloon representing a cartoon dog of your choice. Must be up to Macy's Thanksgiving Day standards," was worth a maximum of 150 points.) But those are in the minority; most items on the List are worth less than 30 points.

The List is distributed to the teams at midnight on the second Wednesday of the month of May. This event is called List Release, and often just getting a copy of the List turns into a minihunt in and of itself. Maybe it will be ensconced in a concrete brick, or buried at the beach. The Judges don't simply hand it over, because in Scav Hunt, nothing is meant to be easy.

Once the team captains have secured copies of the List, they bring them back to their team headquarters for a formal reading of the List, from beginning to end, with the entire team present. The number and size of teams have varied widely over the years. Some years they've been centered around dorms, which means there might be only six or seven teams competing (one for each of the major undergraduate dorms), with up to hundreds of students on each team. Other years, the pendulum has swung toward having many smaller teams, often centered around houses within dorms. Some teams have been based on student clubs (for example, the Astronomical Society once fielded a team), and occasionally a team will be made up of just one person (for example, in 2010, there was Team Lanie, comprising a girl named Lanie).

Once the captains have read the List to their teams, the Scavvies get to work. They spend all of Thursday, Friday, and Saturday completing as many items as they can, sometimes coming together to compete in events like Scav Olympics, Scavenfeast, or the Friday night party. During this time, school remains in session, and some Scavvies go to class, though many do not.

Larger teams have a lot of organization, including page captains: team members in charge of each page of the List, assigning and tracking the completion of the twenty or so items on their page. Teams may also have committees that specifically handle construction items, or coding items, or cooking items. In recent years, many teams have created listhosts and online databases for keeping track of the status of items.

During these three days, a subset of Scavvies head out on the Road Trip. Each team can send a car full of Scavvies—who must be clad in specific and self-referential costumes—to travel around to sites that the Judges have identified and complete location-specific items. This is the part of the Hunt that must occur within a 1,000-mile radius of campus, because at some point somebody determined that 2,000 miles round trip, split among five drivers, was the most anyone should attempt in a three-day time span.

The fourth day of the Hunt, Sunday, is Judgment Day. This coincides with Mother's Day (because mothers are so judgmental). Now is when all the sleep-deprived Scavvies, including the just-returned road-trippers, gather in the campus building Ida Noyes to present their items to the Judges. The Judges assign points to each item, depending on how well it has been completed. The Judges then tabulate the points and announce the final results. The point spread varies from year to year; in 2017, for example, the winning team surpassed 3,500 points, the eighth-place team came in at close to 1,000, and there were a couple of teams who completed just a handful of items and came in under 100 points.

After the results are announced, pretty much everybody cries from exhaustion, cleans up their duct tape and cardboard, bandages whatever injuries they've gained over the past four days, drinks some water, calls their moms to wish them a happy Mother's Day, and completes whatever schoolwork is due the next day. After that, it's just a 361-day wait until we get to do it all again.

All of the stories you are about to read are set during that four-day span. It's just a few days out of the year. But, as you'll see, these are the days when magic can happen.

UNIVERSITY OF CHICAGO STUDENTS PRIDE THEMSELVES on being highly conceptual and deeply impractical. Another school T-shirt reads, "That's all well and good in practice . . . but how does it work in theory?" The U of C offers majors such as "history, philosophy, and social studies of science and medicine" but nothing so applicable as "premed." Even those disciplines that could veer into the hands-on—like "computer science"—are reimagined to be kept firmly in the theoretical realm. On the whole, students at the U of C are extremely intellectual, but that does not necessarily mean that they have much in the way of life skills.

So Scav Hunt is, for many U of C undergrads, the one time of year when they actually make tangible things. Conceptual physicists figure out how to make neon signs and Tesla coils, theoretical economists apply game theory, mathematicians crack codes, and English majors—as in this first essay—learn to solder iron.

ITEM 256:

SIMON'S A COMPUTER, SIMON HAS A BRAIN

Sarah Rosenshine

2007 SCAV HUNT

My Scav Hunt team, Burton-Judson, was not "small but mighty." We were just small. The previous year, my first, we'd come in sixth place. The year before that we'd come in ninth out of nine. However, we always read the List with vigor in a not uncrowded room. And when we read the 2007 List and I heard item 256, I knew it had to be mine. On Team "BJ and the Logical Phalluses," claiming it consisted of the arduous process of announcing, "I'll do that."

256. A. A. A Four. A Four. A Four Trampoline. A Four Trampoline. A Four Trampoline Based. A Four Trampoline Based. A Four Trampoline Based Game. A Four Trampoline Based Game. A Four Trampoline Based Game of. A Four Trampoline Based Game of. A Four Trampoline Based Game of Simon. A Four Trampoline Based Game of BZZZZZZZ. [200 points]

You remember Simon, I assume. It's the handheld circular electronic game with four buttons—red, yellow, green, and blue—that light up in different combinations and then you have to remember and repeat the pattern. The item was asking for a re-creation of that kids' car backseat game—only instead of pressing buttons, you would play by jumping on trampolines.

I waited impatiently the next morning for my friend with a car to return from the Chinese class he'd had the gall to attend. We drove to Target and frantically loaded up his Mini Cooper and debit card with four small trampolines and an even smaller travel Simon game. They were out of the regular Simons, snapped up by Maxcock, our on-the-nose portmanteau for the two largest teams at the time (the dorms Max Palevsky and Snell-Hitchcock). On the ride back, I read the dated slogan off the packaging.

"*Simon's a computer.*

Simon has a brain.

You either do what Simon says or else go down the drain."

"That's weird," I said aloud, even though I was the one riding shotgun in a green Mini Cooper with a Union Jack decal on the roof and four miniature trampolines in the back. As is always the case with Scav, weirdness is relative.

Back on campus I set to work, opening the game with the free screwdriver the university had given all Burton-Judson residents earlier that year. It came with a keychain-sized bubble level and a Snickers bar, by way of apology from the university for months of deafening daytime construction on the dorm. A fair trade.

With YouTube still in its infancy, I turned elsewhere for the very untheoretical knowledge of how circuits work. I called my dad, an inventor who had turned our cavernous basement into a workshop that usually hovers somewhere between *Flubber* and Frankenstein—annoyingly, since as a kid I'd always wanted to turn the basement into a rec room where I could hang out with friends. But today, an inventor father was exactly what I needed.

Fully, if briefly, embodying the absent-minded inventor stereotype, my dad immediately asked why I couldn't get someone from the engineering department to help me.

"You mean from Loyola?" I asked, reminding him that the University of Chicago didn't have anything so practical as an engineering department.

Reality check complete, my dad took apart an orphaned TV remote at home and asked if the circuits matched the look of the board I had in front of me.

"They're squiggly," I reported.

"Good. This one is squiggly, too."

From there, he instructed me to straighten a paper clip and touch it to the ends of the circuit. Hardly believing it could be so simple, despite it being called a "simple circuit," I poked around blindly, touching all the parts one could conceivably call an "end" with the more obvious ends of the paper clip. When the green LED lit up, I did, too. Our captains had been encouraging (pressuring) me to figure out how to make the trampoline Simon work electrically, because doing well on showcase items was the secret to avoiding last place. I wanted to make them happy, but until that point I'd believed I was going to have to make it mechanical, with long Tim Burton-y arms that would hit the Simon buttons when a player bounced. Now I had the literal green light to make the cooler version a reality. From here, I simply needed to solder wires to either end of the circuit, connect those wires to the bottom of the trampoline, and then do that three more times. But first I had to learn how to solder, and also what solder was.

I called home again, where my dad carefully explained how to prevent overmelting by holding the iron near but not on the solder, and I thanked him for his patience by immediately covering an entire circuit with a giant blob. I called back too late that night, my circadian rhythms already replaced with Scavcadian ones, hopeful he could explain how to use wicks, the undo button of the electronics world. Instead, he told me he'd never used them before.

"Oh, because you're so perfect at soldering?" I asked, disheartened.

With time, I figured out I could hold the wick over the solder like a Band-Aid, and it would sop up the solder blood if I held the iron over it. I didn't know much about electrical wiring, but for a hypochondriac, cleaning up blood was second nature.

After more inept soldering and skillful cursing, I finally held in my hands a James Bondian device of splayed wires and exposed circuitry. I took a victory tour of the lounge, looking on as my teammates labored over our Tinkertoy Strandbeest and a fake moon-landing video and our copy of *The Little Engine That Just Couldn't Quite*. Scavving on a small team is like toddlers playing. Working "together" means everyone working on his or her own thing, but sharing supplies and encouragement and watching one another take naps.

After enacting an eighties movie montage of bad ideas, I tried completing the connection between the Simon game and the trampolines with aluminum foil, again barely believing it would work. That first successful bounce, in the early hours of Sunday morning, felt like the highest bounce on the largest trampoline in the world. I excitedly hugged my friends and their friends and people I would never talk to again, reveling in that strange temporary intimacy fostered by extreme situations.

The captains and I carried the game to Judgment, delicately and with great fanfare, like a monarch on a palanquin. Worried we would immediately be shown up, I babbled nervously the whole way. But when I saw my creation in the grass outside Ida with the rest of the Simons, I felt emboldened: aside from the team that smugly announced that theirs used lasers (it didn't), the others were either mechanical or looked a lot like mine.

Simon didn't share my performance anxiety. Though it was a little quiet because I hadn't had time to attach a speaker larger than the built-in one, my most vivid memory is of Judge Claire nodding happily after completing three full bounces. Our team jumped, too, from sixth to fifth that year. That joy buoyed me throughout the day, keeping me smiling even when I was covered in soda, battling bees, after modeling our Coke and Mentos jetpack. I excitedly called my dad from Judgment. He also couldn't believe the aluminum foil had been conductive enough, but he'd always believed I could make Simon work. I packed my tiny screwdriver back into the tiny toolbox, satisfied.

It didn't live there forever, though. Since that Hunt, I have watched my own office slowly turn into a room strewn with half-finished projects, old computers, and tools, with the freebie screwdriver still in rotation. It hasn't reached my dad's Frankenstein levels yet, but I'm getting there.

Horror writer Robert Bloch once said, "I have the heart of a small boy. I keep it in a jar on my desk." Well, I have the brain of a small Simon on mine, and I use it to keep me going on days when I feel my motivation slipping down the drain.

Sarah Rosenshine graduated in 2009 with a degree in English language and literature. She was a Burton-Judson team member for four years, or five if you count overnighting a box of Mallomars from New York to Chicago in 2010 (item 136). She works as a writer, where her writing has appeared in the *Onion*, *McSweeney's*, and the *New Yorker*, and as a software developer, where her work has appeared on the internet.

I WANTED TO START OUT THIS BOOK WITH SARAH'S essay about the four-trampoline Simon game, because it's the story of an item that actually went the way it was supposed to. Sometimes that happens, and it's great. But it is just as likely (if not more so) for an item to go horribly awry, sometimes to the point where the Judges are not only confused or disappointed, but where they wonder why they thought this whole thing would be a good idea in the first place. Sometimes this happens when a team misunderstands an item and very sweetly puts in a lot of effort toward achieving the exact wrong result. Other times this happens when a team purposefully lies or fakes an item in a desperate, low-effort grab for points.

One of the most egregious failed items I ever witnessed as a Judge was one team's "completion" of item 209 from the 2007 List. The item asked for a million dollars in cash, which you've got to admit would be extremely cool to see. The team told us that they had secured this, which sounded remarkable but of course not impossible, because nothing is impossible for Scavvies. They told us that the million dollars was in an armored van and that it would drive past Judgment slowly so that we could see the cash, but it would not stop. We all excitedly gathered on the sidewalk outside of Ida Noyes. A van slowly approached. The windows rolled down. And rather than show us a million dollars in the flesh, the Scavvies inside the van shot at us with water guns.

Needless to say, this received zero points.

Eventually, a word arose to describe these sorts of disappointments. Here, Adam Brozynski tells the story of how he helped define a quintessentially failed item completion.

ITEM 24:

THE TRAINWASH

Adam Brozynski
2010 SCAV HUNT

As Scav teams go, MacPierce was not by any stretch of the imagination what you'd call a powerhouse. We lacked for manpower and materials, and we squandered what little financial resources we had on booze. The highest compliment we'd gotten was when a Judge declared us "adorably janky." MacPierce had little chance of ever winning, but we also had little desire to do so.

It was around 11 p.m. on Saturday night of the 2010 Hunt, and our team headquarters, TANSTAAFL, was abuzz with last-minute item completions.[1] I had just finished putting a Star Destroyer in a bottle for item 231 ("A ship in a bottle. Must be Imperial class or better. [19 BBY points]"), and I was looking for something else to work on when my friend Jasper approached me and said, "Hey, Adam. You doing anything?"

"Nope."

"Cool. I kinda want to do an item that's around twelve points and into which we can put absolutely no effort."

Sounded good to me. We consulted our team's master

---

1. TANSTAAFL was a cafe in the basement of Pierce Tower that also served as MacPierce headquarters. Pronounced just the way it looks, the name is an acronym for "there ain't no such thing as a free lunch," in a nod to famed U of C economist Milton Friedman. TANSTAAFL was permanently closed in 2011 due to a rat infestation, yet continued to serve as Scav HQ until Pierce Tower was demolished in 2013. Maybe Scavvies should be deterred by rats, but we're not.

copy of the List: sixteen sheets of paper affixed in two uneven rows to a bare brick wall. After several abortive attempts (item 49: "Ballistic press-on nails: fingernails that can be fired from your hands to vaguely annoy attackers! [5 points]") proved to be too much of an engineering challenge to satisfy our "absolutely no effort" criterion, we came across this gem:

24. That train is looking pretty grimy. Do me a favor and ride it through a drive-through trainwash. [12 points]

Now, we might have been fourth-place contenders on a good day, but we weren't idiots. Of course it occurred to us that somewhere in the great city of Chicago there might be a location where actual trains are actually cleaned. It also occurred to us that the Judges probably wanted us to find such a location and ride a train through it. But, frankly, that's not what we were about that night. So we chose to ignore those facts. We were going to make our own train and clean it in our own way.

"How can we make something that vaguely resembles a train?" is one of those questions that you only ever find yourself asking during Scav. "How can we make something that vaguely resembles a train using only the materials within fifty feet of us?" is a question you only ever find yourself asking during Scav and less than twelve hours before Judgment. As MacPierce, naturally we had very few materials within fifty feet of us, but we *did* have a shopping cart.

For the benefit of my readers who have never seen a train before (and if you saw the final product of this item, you would certainly place me in that category), we settled on the following qualities as being hallmarks of a train: a train is opaque, not grated like a shopping cart; a train has a cow catcher in front; a train has wheels; a train has a smokestack. Simple enough, right?

Our first step was to cover the shopping cart in trash bags. In retrospect I'm not sure why this was necessary, but it seemed vitally important at the time. We found a half-broken crate for the cow catcher and a bucket for the smokestack. For some reason we put the smokestack at the back of the train.

As I reflect on this process, I don't recall either of us ever actually looking at a picture of a train.

Finally, we needed some wheels. Fortunately, in the same room was a fellow Scavvie working on item 84 who could spare a couple of balloons. (Item 84, for the curious: "Balloon animals are for those clowns in the social sciences! I want a balloon protein, one that both represents your chosen protein's tertiary/quaternary structure and actively demonstrates its native function. Like a real protein, your structure should be sufficiently complex and, most importantly, do something cool (none of that occludin-β bullshit). [50 points]")

So we blew up a couple of those long balloon-animal balloons, bent them into circles, and decided that would suffice for wheels.

At that point, someone entered TANSTAAFL and asked us, "Are you guys making a train?" That was all we needed. Someone had, unprompted, positively identified our shopping cart as a train. We immediately ceased construction.

This process had exhausted us. Somehow it had taken two hours to quasi-transform a shopping cart. Now, come hell or high water, we were going to wash this train.

Having only the meager resources allotted to us by the dorm, we opted to wash our train in the communal shower. Jasper and I recruited some first years to help film this endeavor. One particularly brave individual volunteered to strip to his underwear and ride the "train" through the shower.

And so we and the train piled into the elevator and headed up to the third-floor bathroom. One of our balloon wheels popped in transit. We decided not to replace it.

We arrived at the third-floor shower, our team's only video camera in hand. Our first year disrobed and mounted

the shopping cart. I decided that the best way to convey
the facts that (a) this was a train and (b) we were cleaning it
would be to have the rest of us, standing off-camera, prod
the shopping cart with brooms and mops and make train
noises. A lengthy debate followed about how many times we
should say "chugga" before each "choo-choo." (I will contend
until my dying breath that eight is the proper number.) That
dispute was left unresolved, so in the final filming each person just said as many "chugga"s as they thought proper. We
recorded a thirty-second video punctuated by a triumphal
cry of "this train is so clean!" and called it a wrap.

One of our captains that year, Rafael, presented that
page to the Judges the next day. We did not tell Rafael how
we had completed this particular item. We simply sent him
the file and assured him it was perfect.

The look on the Judge's face upon seeing this video is
best described as "crestfallen." I don't think Rafael was too
impressed, either. Needless to say, we received no points.

But our completion of this item was not entirely in vain.
I was elected captain of MacPierce the following year, largely
on a pro-trainwash platform. It became an inside joke on
our team: a "trainwashed" item was a low-effort completion that flagrantly defied the Judges' expectations. By 2015,
"trainwash" had entered the broader Scav lexicon.

Two years after this incident, a friend met the trainwash Judge at a party, and the Judge shared his thoughts on
the item: "You know, I really love Scav. I've never seriously
thought about quitting being a Judge . . . except for that one
time when your team showed me that trainwash video."

In my defense, though, that train was so clean.

Adam Brozynski majored in physics and graduated in 2012. He Scavved
with MacPierce and was a team captain in 2011 and 2012. He currently
lives in New York City, where he works as a software engineer.

THERE'S A LINE IN ADAM BROZYNSKI'S "TRAINWASH" essay that could be said about the majority of what participants do for Scav Hunt:

"In retrospect I'm not sure why this was necessary, but it seemed vitally important at the time."

In this way, Scav Hunt is just the nerdier version of more commonplace college traditions (like rushing a sorority or performing organized cheers at football games): out of context, this behavior is inexplicable, but within the community, no other option is imaginable. Scavvies know that they don't *have* to cover a shopping cart with garbage bags in the same way that fraternity members know they don't *have* to do a keg stand. But they go all in nonetheless, because the group is counting on them, because it's part of their identities, because it's tradition.

How did Scav reach this rarified standing after its origins as a vaguely normal collegiate activity? In this next essay, one of the creators of the first Hunt provides some backstory on how we got here.

ITEM 175:

THE FIRST HUNT

Diane A. Kelly

1987 SCAV HUNT

Compared to the elaborate items Scav has challenged teams to obtain over the years, an aluminum soda can seems ordinary, ubiquitous, some might say *boring*. But the efforts teams made to get their hands on one during the first Scavenger Hunt ultimately inspired one of the event's longest-running traditions.

In the fall of 1986, Chris Straus had come up with the idea of running a scavenger hunt on campus during May's "Summer Breeze," the university's annual arts festival. I was recruited to his team of organizers when my friend Cassie Scharff poked her head into my room and said, "Hey Diane, we're going to plan a scavenger hunt, and you should help!" At the time, I was struggling to juggle a work-study job at the Regenstein with the most challenging classes I'd ever faced, but I said yes anyway. I loved games, and this sounded like it could be even more fun than the string of raucous Assassin games I'd run in the halls between classes in high school.

So from then on, I joined a small group of Chris's friends and friends-of-friends around a table in the Reynolds Club every week, spitballing ideas for items and figuring out how we were going to run this thing.

We really had no idea what we were doing.

Our "meetings" were mostly just us trying to make one another laugh. Whatever made us laugh hardest went down on the List. I don't remember which one of us first brought up the fact that Illinois didn't make you pay a deposit on soda cans, but it didn't take long for that idle observation to turn into "What if we made teams drive somewhere that does?" Everyone thought Michigan and its ten-cent deposit was too easy to get to, so we settled on a version that would require a bit more effort:

175. A 5-cent returnable soda can (hint: Try Iowa, New Hampshire, Conn., Vermont) [100 points]

And then we didn't think about it again until Judgment Day, when we started to hear stories. Not that we paid a lot of attention to them in the moment—we were far too busy dealing with the consequences of inadequate planning.

I said we had no idea what we were doing, right? Well, it showed. We'd reserved a room on the third floor of Ida Noyes that was far too small for all the teams that arrived that day. (We'd offered every team that participated a coupon for a free ice cream social, which in retrospect may have goosed turnout.) We'd planned for each Judge to go over the entire List's items one team at a time, so the 5-to-1 team-to-Judge ratio left lots of teams crammed in that overstuffed room for hours, cooling their heels until one of us got to them. We didn't have a plan to tabulate points on the fly over the course of the day, which left us working late into the night to figure out who had won the prize money for first place. (Chamberlin House, by the way. Whole-dorm megateams were still far in the future.)

As we desperately worked to get through everyone's items, a lot of participants took the time to tell us about the adventures they'd had that weekend. And that's when we realized how memorable that boring soda can item had become.

Hitchcock's team had driven all the way to Iowa to buy a couple of six-packs while listening to a tape of *American Pie* on repeated loop to write down its lyrics (item 170: "The complete lyrics for 'American Pie,' by Don McLean. [5 points]"). Another team convinced a member whose father worked for one of the major airlines to go to O'Hare and use their "free family travel" perk to fly standby to New York City, drop a bunch of quarters into an airport soda machine, and immediately fly back to Chicago, cans in hand.

It showed a level of devotion to the game we hadn't expected. And that's part of what inspired us to plan the *second* annual Scavenger Hunt.

For the 1988 Hunt, we figured out ways to fix our biggest problems. We reserved the entire ground floor of Ida Noyes for Judgment Day, where it remains today. We streamlined the judging process by putting each Judge in charge of one page of the List and circulating them around the teams, so no team had to wait too long before a Judge showed up to look at part of their stash. We kept a running point tally going throughout the day, so we could figure out team rankings within a couple of hours after judging ended. And we created the position of "Head Judge," which mercifully gave the most argumentative team captains a single target for their complaints.

And we got a *lot* more ambitious with the List. We started asking teams to *create* items instead of simply finding them. We embedded a gift to the community into the List by asking teams to donate blood for points. And that humble soda can? Well, we decided that if teams were willing to drive to Iowa for one item, we could ask them to drive a *lot* farther to hunt down a carload of them. Canada? Graceland? Duluth? Road Trip!

By the time I took off on my own one-way road trip to graduate school, I had judged four Hunts and, through them, gained a group of lifelong friends, met the man I later married, and helped create something that more than thirty years later I'm still delighted by and proud of. My first instincts were right: Scav Hunt was—and still is—a ton of fun.

Diane A. Kelly helped plan and judge Scav from 1987 to 1990, before graduating from the College with a degree in biological sciences. She is now a biologist and science writer living in western Massachusetts. You can read about her work at dianeakelly.com.

ONE OF THE BIGGEST EXTERNAL FACTORS TO CHANGE
Scav since the first Hunt, which Diane Kelly describes, has been the rise of the internet. It's provided teams with much more complex organizational structures, it's given rise to countless meme-based items, and it's made any item that can be answered by a simple Google search now completely irrelevant. Back in those premodern days of the Hunt, here are some of the items that teams would spend hours researching.

12 TRIVIA ITEMS THAT WERE CHALLENGING IN THE AGE BEFORE GOOGLE

1987.159: Whose home is the exterior of Mandel Hall modeled after? [10 points]

> Mandel Hall, the university's main concert hall, was a gift to the young University of Chicago by department store tycoon Leon Mandel. It is modeled after the great hall of Crosby House, built in 1472 by Sir John Crosby, Sheriff of London.

1996.340: Why did Northwestern's main library start to sink into the ground? [2 points]

> Urban legend has it that, while designers had properly accounted for the weight of the building, they did not account for the weight of the books.

1988.106: What unusual thing did Jay Berwanger do with his Heisman trophy before he gave it to the University? [7 points]

> Jay Berwanger was the first winner of the Heisman Trophy, in 1935. Before his donation, he used the trophy as a doorstop, both in his library and to keep the front door open while visiting his Aunt Gussie.

1992.6: How was I. W. Colburn connected with the UofC? [1 point]

He was the "architectural consultant" for the University of Chicago.

1990.33: What happened in Rome on Oct. 10, 1582? [6 points]

Since the switch from the Julian to the Gregorian calendar meant that days leapt from October 4 to October 15, nothing at all happened!

1994.41: Who was the college roommate of Indiana Jones at the University of Chicago, according to "The Young Indiana Jones Chronicles"? [2 points]

As revealed in "Chapter 20: The Mystery of the Blues," Indiana's roommate was Eliot Ness.

1992.109: How did firemen try to prevent Daniel Goodwin from ascending the John Hancock Tower in November 1981? [3 points]

On November 11, 1981, Daniel Goodwin climbed the John Hancock Tower in Chicago dressed as Spider-Man, supposedly to call attention to deficiencies in fire-rescue plans for skyscrapers. The fire department, on the inside of the building, used fire axes to shatter window glass near Goodwin and then, through the openings in the glass, attempted to dislodge Goodwin from the building with grappling hooks attached to long poles.

1991.21: Correctly complete this quote describing the U of C: "the greatest collection of _____ since _____." [6 points]

A. J. Liebling in his book *The Second City* described the University of Chicago as "the greatest collection of juvenile neurotics since the Children's Crusade."

1993.76: Da Bears own the record for the worst thrashing ever handed out to another NFL team. Who did they beat and by how much? [1 point]

> In December 1940, the Chicago Bears beat the Washington Redskins 73–0.

1995.240: What are the ingredients in the shaving cream of Shaving Fun Ken™ doll? [2 points]

> Deionized water, stearic acid, sorbitol, petrolatum, glyceryl stearate, peg-100 stearate, isopropyl mystristate, mineral oil, triethanolamine, methylparaben, and phenoxyethanol.

1993.12: What is best in life? [1 point]

> As Conan the Barbarian could tell you, "To crush your enemies, see them driven before you, and to hear the lamentations of their women!"

1994.43: What book is recorded by ISBN 0-8362-1735-7? [5 points]

> Bill Watterson's Calvin and Hobbes treasury *The Days Are Just Packed*. And during Scav, the days certainly are.

AT FOUR DAYS, 300-PLUS ITEMS, HUNDREDS UPON HUN-
dreds of participants, and a thirty-year history of building vending
machines, zeusaphones, and the like, it should go without saying
that Scav Hunt is the world's largest scavenger hunt. But, as it
turns out, *nothing* goes without saying. In 2011, Scav decided to
prove its claim to fame. Here's what happened.

ITEM Z77:

THE WORLD'S LARGEST SCAVENGER HUNT

Ezra Deutsch-Feldman

2011 SCAV HUNT

1.

I remember the day that the 1996 *Guinness Book of World Records* arrived at my elementary school. I had only just that morning been looking at my pencil, sharpened and shortened almost to the point of nonexistence, and wondered, "Could this be the shortest pencil in the world?"

If you think of the *Guinness Book of World Records* and imagine a coffee-table book sporting a holographic cover, filled with color photos, and set up in a large display table near the checkout line at Barnes and Noble, that's not what I got that day. This was before the book was so flashy, back when it was a short, fat paperback full of densely packed text, carefully describing the largest, smallest, fastest, slowest, and all other superlative feats ever recorded. The record holders were listed with almost no context or explanation. And I wanted to be in it.

I didn't really care what record I had, but I wanted something. With all the careful planning you would expect from an eight-year-old, I began brainstorming the various achievements I thought were possible. Perhaps I could create the world's biggest sandwich. Or wear a watch for the longest time. Or, finding one record on the list that seemed particularly easy to beat, I could amass the world's largest collection of traffic cones. None of these, of course, came close to happening, and as I grew up, I slowly let go of my dream to get in the record books.

2.

The University of Chicago Scavenger Hunt has been calling itself the world's largest scavenger hunt since at least 2002, but it wasn't until 2011, the year of the twenty-fifth hunt, that we decided to make it official. Judge Daniel Citron had started researching Guinness's rules and guidelines and spearheaded our efforts to break the record. At the time, the record was held by a group of 212 students at St. Anthony's Catholic School in Ontario. We could easily beat 212! Some Scav teams were bigger than that on their own!

Scav has always loved world's largest items, usually in the form of roadside attractions. Just the previous year I had seen the world's largest tire in Michigan while on the Judge Road Trip, and we've had Scavvies visit all serious claimants to the title of world's largest ball of twine.

But those are physical objects, simple to measure. When you sit down and try to officially break the record for world's largest scavenger hunt, you soon realize that a "scavenger hunt" is a slippery idea, and measuring the size of one is even trickier. Scav has always prided itself on the length of each year's List, usually 270–330 items. But just making a long list can't be the measure of how big the hunt actually is, because a list is just words on paper. The question is, how many people will actually *work* on completing those items?

But just the number of participants isn't a good solution either—if that were the case, you could have had a pregame "scavenger hunt" with the 108,000 people in the crowd at the world's most attended basketball game by asking everyone in the crowd to look for, say, a shiny penny, and then you'd have just organized a scavenger hunt with over a hundred thousand people.

And don't get me started on length of time—I'll break that record right now. Go find me a "Richard Nixon for President" button. Meet me in Ida Noyes for Judgment before the time limit runs out, which is one thousand years from now. Congratulations, you've just embarked on the world's largest scavenger hunt (as measured in days).

3.

Here's what the people at Guinness ended up with for their definition of a scavenger hunt:

—The event must take place in a defined physical location with clear entrances and exits;
—There must be teams of exactly four players each;
—The event must last at least one hour.

In other words, they are describing something *completely different* from the University of Chicago Scavenger Hunt. Judge Daniel proposed that we break the record by holding a scavenger-hunt-within-a-scavenger-hunt, as an outdoor event on Friday evening. Teams would get points for the University of Chicago Scav Hunt by turning out to participate in the Guinness World Record scavenger hunt, which would have its own list and scoring system.

To some Judges, there was a little bit of fuzzy logic to this arrangement. If the only thing that's being counted is one hour of Friday night, would it *really* be our Scav Hunt that held the record? As far as Guinness was concerned, the University of Chicago Scavenger Hunt would be a one-hour event and wouldn't include any of the other 276 items on the List that year. Would the record be held by *the* University of Chicago Scavenger Hunt? Or just a scavenger hunt that was *at* the University of Chicago?

Furthermore, did we really need the validation of Guinness World Records to know that we were the largest scavenger hunt in the world? We considered our record-holding status as self-evident, and we had never needed official recognition before. Who cares what a bunch of beer-slinging record keepers think? Wasn't our founding principle that chaos is freedom? Don't we pride ourselves on making a mockery of authority in all forms?

In the end we decided to go for it. We looked past those issues, just as I personally avoided thinking too much about the fact that I wouldn't actually be *participating* in the record-breaking event myself, just helping to organize and run it along with the other Judges. And I wasn't even a particularly central figure in organizing it; that credit goes to Daniel Citron and that year's Head Judge, Grace Chapin. But I knew it was certainly the closest I was going to get to my childhood dream, so I was all in.

4.

277. And now, let's talk seriously for a moment. We've been together for 25 years now, and we think it's time to make it official. On Friday evening, at 5:30 p.m., come to the University Avenue entrance to the Quads to set a new world record for the largest scavenger hunt. [Δ points]

Here's how the event worked. Teams showed up on the quads, signed in, and got a wristband (this was part of the Guinness requirements to make sure we were very careful about counting exactly how many people were involved). Everyone got a list, to be opened when the event began at 6:30. As required, we had impartial bystanders and media on hand to double-check our numbers and confirm that all rules were being followed.

After Daniel explained the rules once more, he gave the signal, and the event (and its one-hour countdown) began. Most items could be completed by walking around the quads and answering questions based on campus buildings, plaques, and statues. A few required interacting with Judges in some way. Once the Scavvies were off and running, we Judges switched from set-up-and-register mode to end-things-and-collect-the-answers mode. As the final minutes and seconds ticked down, a larger and larger crowd of Scavvies was amassing at Hutch Courtyard, where they turned in their answer sheets and we explained how the rest of the logistics worked. We had promised the participants ice cream afterward, since apparently just breaking a world record wasn't quite enough incentive. I got to explain this to them, since I have a pretty loud voice, and it was a very large group of people. After I was done, just for good measure, I added, "THIS IS THE LOUDEST I HAVE EVER BEEN!" (So count that as at least one personal record broken that day.)

As the ice cream line slowly moved along, the Judges were inside, grading the answer sheets as quickly as we could. As it happens, the winners were from the incredibly small Team Rural Juror, which actually only had one person on campus to work on items (that one participant roped in three friends so he could participate in the event). The prizes were copies of the DVD *Scavengers,* a documentary made a couple years before about the 2007 Hunt. (It's a very good movie, even if I've never forgiven the directors for cutting my one line out of it.) Team Rural Juror got precious few points that weekend beyond what they earned on Friday night.

After that, we did our best to clean up and moved on to

the rest of the Hunt. After all, there were other events and hundreds of other items to work on before Judgment started.

5.

After Scav ended, Judge Daniel got all the documentation together to send to Guinness. They make it suspiciously difficult to meet all their documentation requirements— unless, that is, you pay several thousand dollars for their own representatives to be at your event.

Actually, Guinness World Records gives you ample op- portunities to send them money. They've changed quite a lot since the days of my humble 1996 edition. Right around the time the book switched over to being a print equivalent of a Ripley's Believe It or Not! tourist trap, they started hosting their records online. The books became a sort of a yearly best-of publication rather than a complete reference guide. This is also when they changed their name from The Guin- ness Book of World Records to just Guinness World Records.

Without the space limitations of a physical book, the number of records they could keep track of skyrocketed. Ac- cording to the Guinness website, their books contained about 4,000 records, while the website tracks 40,000. That means there are 36,000 records that simply didn't exist before the internet. And believe me, there are some pretty ridiculous things on there. If it's true that the book was originally created to settle bar fights, I doubt very much that those Guinness drinkers were arguing over the most magic tricks performed in a single skydive. Or the longest line of strudels. Or fastest iron bar bending to fit into a suitcase.

Why do these records exist? Well, the answer is right at the top of the Guinness website: Under the heading "Busi- ness Solutions," they suggest that you "use our brand to reach your audience." Their news page hosts press releases from dozens of brands that have held a record-breaking attempt as a publicity stunt. Guinness more or less admits that it's all a sham when they tell prospective clients that "the unique flexibility of our record titles means that we can develop campaigns firmly aligned to your objectives." Someone already beat you to the longest line of strudels? Well, maybe your company can try longest line of apple pies instead. Sorry, longest line of hot dogs has already been taken.

Of course, there are application fees for all of these records. Optional judges, event planning, marketing, memorabilia, and even participation certificates will all make your event smoother and more successful, and Guinness is more than happy to sell you all of them.

6.

But I didn't know any of that yet. All I knew was that we had smashed the previous record, with Daniel telling us the final count was a whopping 924 participants (231 teams of four people each), well over four times the number St. Anthony's Catholic School in Ontario had been able to muster.

We waited weeks, then months, for our record to be published online. Finally, we had our moment: "The largest scavenger hunt consisted of 924 participants and was organised by the University of Chicago Scavenger Hunt at the University of Chicago's campus in Chicago, Illinois, USA, on 6 May 2011." The certificate came in the mail. It was beautiful. We all admired it, with enormous pride that there could now be no doubt: the annual event we took such pride in was now the world's largest, officially. It was widely agreed that the children at St. Anthony's would be crying in their maple syrup when they heard the news.

We had managed to beat the record, and we did it without giving Guinness a cent more than we had to. We didn't

have to compromise what Scav is, and the event didn't de-
tract from the "real" Hunt in any way. And, of course, I was
thrilled. It may never have seen a printed page, and my name
may not have been on it—in fact, the other Judges and I
didn't even count as part of the 924 people—but I considered it a childhood dream I could finally check off, long after
having given up on it.

7.

And so it lasted for several years. But the corporate monster
that is Guinness World Records continued its scheme, par-
laying its decades of respect as a beloved reference book into,
essentially, a glorified PR firm. In retrospect, it's surprising
that we held the record as long as we did. Three years later,
we got word that there was an upcoming attempt to break
our record. And it was backed by a corporate juggernaut
even the legendary Scav Hunt Judges couldn't beat: Google.

Yes, Google—specifically their Google Fiber internet
service—was about to be introduced to the town of Provo,
Utah. The town was organizing a scavenger hunt to pro-
mote it, as part of an event called "Passport to Provo." I was
heartbroken, but I could see no possible way we would
keep the record. It was clear that Guinness had pulled out
all the stops for Google, including sending representatives
to the event (presumably costing Google tens of thousands
of dollars), and even allowed some fudging of the rules to
accommodate the good people of Provo (allowing the list
and items to be published ahead of time, to let people plan
their strategy).

I waited with dread as the day arrived, trying to hold
out hope of a massive rainstorm, a sudden loss of interest
in internet access among the people of Provo, or even some
kind of unexpected sabotage from a group of two hundred

Canadian schoolchildren who just so happened to show up in town.

But it didn't help. On September 13, 2014, the city of Provo got 2,079 people to participate in its event. A number of people, I note, that is suspiciously not divisible by four.

But what had we lost, exactly? Guinness is no longer really a collection of records; it's just a collection of people who had a couple thousand dollars to spare for an unusual form of advertising. When everyone in the world can be a record breaker, it becomes a lot less special. Not only was I not in the book, even if I got in, it wouldn't have any meaning. Achieving the dream I had back in elementary school, when I held my 1996 *Guinness Book of World Records*, was no longer just *practically* impossible for me, it was *conceptually* impossible, like wanting to visit a historic building only to find out it's been demolished.

8.

I remembered something from the 2010 Judge Road Trip, right after we saw the world's largest tire. We visited a farm with a small museum next door, and the owner told us he had the world's largest pulley on display. It was pretty large, we all agreed, and the phrase "world's largest" certainly got our attention. Did he have proof? "Well, have you ever seen a bigger one?" he asked us in reply. None of us had. That was evidence enough for him, and we had to admit it was evidence enough for us, too.

As I headed back to Chicago the following spring, the people of Provo were doing . . . nothing. Their scavenger hunt was just a distant memory. Ours was still coming up, just like it would be the next May, and the May after that. None of the Scavvies or Judges screaming and cheering in Ida Noyes Hall on that Wednesday night before Mother's Day seemed

to mind that Guinness had taken away our official designa-
tion. As far as we were concerned, the event we were about
to begin, for the twenty-ninth year in a row, was the world's
largest scavenger hunt. Always has been, always will be.

◇◇

Ezra Deutsch-Feldman was in the University of Chicago's class of 2010
and graduated with a degree in political science. He lived in Pierce Tower
and was a member of the MacPierce Scav Hunt team from 2007 to 2009,
including two years as a captain. He became a Judge in 2010. He now
works in politics.

DOING THINGS THE BIGGEST, THE BEST, OR IN ANY WAY

the most excessive is core to Scav's identity. There is no Guinness World Record for highest-pointed Scav Hunt item, but if there were, these would be some of the contenders.

23 OF THE HIGHEST-POINTED SCAV HUNT ITEMS OF ALL TIME

1987.91: A Dean. [30 points] A gagged and bound person. [30 points] A nude, gagged, and bound Dean. [500 points]

1988.172: A crouton. [100 points]

> One of the things that led to the early popularity of Scav Hunt was how any team that scored more than 100 points would be granted a five-gallon tub of ice cream from the Maroon Market. Which, as you can see, was relatively easy to accomplish for anyone who actually read the list.

1991.162: A motor or sail boat at least 25 feet from stem to stern, with ownership papers and certificate of inspection by government authorities. † [300 points]

> One team managed to get a pretty awesome cigarette boat with the papers and everything, scoring full points. Another team glued twenty-five tiny Barbie feet to the bottom of a toy boat. Which got fewer points.

1993.57: A fully functional Soviet military aircraft with receipt (we suggest a MIG, they're on sale). [1999.99 points]

1994.213: An authentic space suit. (The kind astronauts could use on a space walk) [100 points]

1995.34: A mobile staircase used to board passengers onto a large commercial airplane (we want the real thing) [180 points]

2000.223: The True Monster of the Midway. Choose a classic monster (Godzilla, Patrick Bateman, King Kong) and construct him in monstrous size on the Midway, or, rather, the Quad. Size counts both in height and footprint. We want something sturdy (more "I want this in my statuary" than "I want this in my bullshit collection of cardboard cutouts"), and no inflatable monkeys that you rented from a car dealership. Don't embarrass yourself with something not even 8 meters tall. [350 points]

2002.80: "The wind bloweth where it listest, and thou hearest the sound thereof, but canst not tell whence it cometh, and wither it goeth: so is everyone that is born of the Spirit." Construct for us, please, a molen of extraordinary magnitude. We would love a standaardmolen, a wipmolen or even a kloeke poldermolen, but we'd also be plenty happy with a stellingmolen or even a paltrok. Your molen should resemble that in which Ash took his ill-fated refuge, or perhaps even the (far less cool) molen from *Chitty Chitty Bang Bang*. This molen should be approximately 2:1 in scale, and can also be used as an obstacle for Item 2002.98. Since the Midway has already been quite thoroughly drained, and we get our 'lectricity from them outlets, your molen should function such that, when rotating, 1 cup of dried corn can be ground into a fine meal. [425 points. 25 bonus points if, with its thin wasp-waist, your molen looks like a dainty, gay damsel which, brightening up the whole landscape, is a pleasure to behold. And we changed our minds: 100 bonus points if it can actually drain the Midway and reclaim some land for dear old UofC, considering the space crunch and wet weather we've been having lately]

> "Molens" are more commonly known as windmills.
> 2002.98 was a U of C–themed miniature golf course.

2003.138: Build us a functioning pinball machine. [200 points. 20

bonus points if it is coin operated. 40 bonus points if it is themed after *Flight of the Navigator*. 60 bonus points if a Judge gets multi-ball and the high score. TILT bonus points if, after that, a deaf, dumb, and blind member of your team beats the high score, and no one can help noticing that he "sure plays a mean pinball"]

2004.160: The biggest goddamn sombrero we've ever seen. Fully functional sombreros only. [12 points per square foot. No goddamn limit. 6 bonus points for a goddamn running rendition of the Mexican Hat dance]

> On the night prior to Judgment Day, Judges learned that at least three teams hoped to earn over a thousand points with their giant sombreros. After a heated discussion, Judges tentatively decided to honor the item as pointed, albeit stressing the "fully functional" modifier. In the end, the top prize for this item was 594 points given to Pierce for an authentic-looking papier-mâché sombrero accompanied by a graceful hat dance. And the Judges vowed never to include the phrase "no goddamn limit" on any item ever again.

2004.268: Build a tesla coil and broadcast energy to an area on the Midway. Power a vibrator, a lava lamp, and a Theremin, with the mad Martian's radiant juice. [201 points]

2006.52: A walk-in kaleidoscope. [200 points]

> Max Palevsky's team earned an additional five points by invoking 2006.267, which required the use of a trampoline in conjunction with any other item on the list. Why every amusement park does not feature a mini trampoline inside of a walk-in kalei-doscope, I do not know.

2007.234: A walking, working, people-powered but preferably wind-powered Strandbeest. [300 points]

> These wacky wooden walking machines were originally created by Dutch artist Theo Jansen. The best completions walked themselves to Judgment.

2008.22: A wicker phallus. Size matters. [2 points per foot, no fucking limit]

> It did not take long for the Judges to forget the lessons of the biggest goddamn sombrero.

2009.209: Build a vending machine. Vending machines must be coin operated, with multiple button-selected options to choose from. In addition to whatever sugary goodness you choose, machines must vend three other List items when you type in their item numbers. [250 points]

2011.79: A Trojan vertebrate containing at least two (adult human) team members. Note: the Judges have grown wise to your wiles over the past few millennia and are likely to spurn another Trojan® horse or Trojan rabbit. [125 points, or 0 points if your Trojan vertebrate is limbless]

2011.241: Hey kids! At Jack's Tavern, buy your very own ball of twine starter kit, and say hello to the newest member of the Cabinet. Over the course of the next two days, you will add to the ball of twine and nurture it. Document its growth by having it present in all subsequent road trip photos. Top it off with the flag and sign from the starter kit, and bring your buddy to Judgment. [6 points for the starter kit, 0.1 points per cubic inch]

> Here's the thing about the volume of spheres: those exponents start paying off really fast, and the MacPierce team stood to get hundreds of points

for an admittedly impressively large ball. (People in twine ball country take it as a point of pride to have a lot of it on hand to provide to visitors.)

2012.264: King's Landing and The Twins are all right, I guess, but we'd rather see something a little more neo-Gothic. Produce a map of the UofC campus that when triggered erects a clockwork version of a campus building of your choice. [175 points]

> A reference to the title sequence for *Game of Thrones*, successful completions of this item had models of U of C buildings rising out of the ground.

2014b.140: We've long been told that books can transport us to faraway places. We'd like one that actually delivers on this promise. Construct a pop-up book large enough for us to explore the whimsical and well-engineered structures within. Multiple pages would be nice, but we're really just after one fantastic centerfold. [150 points]

2015.190: A University of Chicago–themed one-armed bandit. That's right: an RSO funding slot machine for those of us annually cowering before the CLI. Must be mechanical (not video) and have at least three reels producing differentiated outcomes. Must be homemade and may not actually accept or dispense legal tender. Must have a dizzying amount of lights and sounds. [200 points]

> These abbreviations are just an insider-y way of talking about how much funding an extracurricular club gets from the university.

2016.82: Your RH is coming to your room for a chat, but your desk is still littered with those detailed plans for throwing things out the window, plus various other bits of contraband! Not to worry! You've rigged a single switch to make at least four parts of your desk flip, slide, or otherwise vanish from sight, to be replaced with less incriminating facades. [200 points]

"RH" refers to "Resident Head."

2017.44: Rotate, turn, circle, spin, twirl, whirl, pirouette, and twist. That's what your small carousel, capable of riding two Judges and fitting within a square fathom, will do. And it will be themed on something else that rotates, turns, circles, spins, twirls, whirls, pirouettes, or twists. [200 points]

2017.178: Some people like to collect souvenir snow globes from around the world, but for us, looking at a 2"-diameter sphere from the outside isn't quite intimate enough. Construct a snow globe inside of which a Judge can comfortably explore an intricate scene from any world city. We don't care about how your snow globe looks externally, but we do expect internal enhancements such as lights, moving parts, and flurries of snow. [150 points]

WHAT MAKES A GOOD SCAV HUNT ITEM? JUDGES CAN
argue over this endlessly; indeed, conversations that start out as simply "Would 'a gun' be a good item?" often turn into way-too-long philosophical debates about what the "point" of Scav Hunt is.

To my mind, what makes for a good item is a combination of being (a) achievable and (b) if achieved, a cool experience for the Scavvie who completes it and/or the Judge who judges it.

So, in my opinion, "Alter the face of the Moon permanently" (item 278, 2000) was not a good item because it can't be done.

And an item like number 15 of 2001, which required Scavvies to copy in lead pencil the entirety (or as far as they could get) of the 1961 reprint of the *Oxford English Dictionary*, also strikes me as not a good item. Because, while it is achievable, it is boring for the Scavvies to do and boring to judge.

Obviously, some Judges disagree with me on this or these items wouldn't have made it on to the List in the first place. Some Judges love including impossible items, or items that are super time-consuming and unrewarding for the Scavvies. The argument in favor of these Sisyphean items is that they are the ultimate equalizer. It doesn't matter if you're a well-funded team or not; you can't buy your way out of a long memorization or repetitious item.

And sometimes Judges simply disagree about what a "cool experience" looks like. For me, Scavvies racing to eat bowls of fish food (2003, Scav Olympics item 7) is disgusting for all involved. For others, watching people choke down fish flakes is what they live for.

When deciding whether or not to include an item on the List, Judges sometimes have to balance these two core criteria of being both achievable and rewarding. So if something is *very* hard to achieve but would be *very* cool if managed, it's still a good item.

Occasionally the Judges pass an item on the belief that it's achievable when in fact it's not—an example of this being item 25 from 2006: "A sunblocker, the likes of which will cause every plant and tree to die and owls to deafen us with their incessant hooting [300 points per city block that is cast into eternal darkness]." Sure, the Judges knew this was unlikely to happen. But they asked for it anyway because *wouldn't it be cool if it did?* And that is the category into which this next item falls.

ITEM 240:

THE HOMEMADE BREEDER REACTOR

Fred Niell

1999 SCAV HUNT

240. A breeder reactor built in a shed, and the boy scout badge to prove credit was given where boy scout credit was due. [500 points]

It was spring quarter 1999. Justin Kasper and I were roommates and physics majors, and we had just sent our acceptances to graduate school. We were looking forward to coasting for the last three months of college and we weren't really concentrating on our studies. We were too busy . . . "accessing" the physics department after hours for our assorted nefarious purposes.

Once I assembled a 1.2GW (that's right, gigawatt) pulse power system for—well, let's be honest. It was for blowing stuff up. Justin (J for short) and I had stolen some parts and bought others, used the machine shop at all hours, and basically hewn this thing from the primordial forces of nature herself. It was amazing, and in the following weeks we blew up whatever we could get our hands on. We vaporized apples and made water explode like dynamite. We were gods in the lab from eleven at night until six in the morning. We cleared out before any of the staff arrived to open up.

We were misbehaving, but not in a malevolent way. We were applying what we had learned in our advanced lab classes in a practical setting. In essence, we were being good experimentalists. The faculty may even have known this, but plausible deniability, in the words of one of my favorite physicists, goes a long way.

This paradise, this Eden of partying and blowing stuff up for class credit while breaking as many university rules as possible, lasted for a few months. Then the 1999 Scav Hunt came along.

Initially, I wasn't interested in putting much time or effort into Scav that year. I was by then working full time at the Fermilab, a Department of Energy national lab near Chicago specializing in high-energy particle physics, while also taking a full load of those core classes I was supposed to have already finished. Every night I brought home cheap beer, and J and I blasted techno from our embarrassingly large and complex stereo system and threw parties in our dorm room. Cocktail parties and Tuesday parties and "day-of-the-week-ending-in-Y" parties. Why would I plug into the frenetic energy required by the Hunt when I was already burning the candle at both ends and dousing it with gasoline? On the night of List Release, I skipped the midnight reading. I went downtown instead and had some fun with my friends.

The next morning, in the dining hall, I was minding my own business (working the newspaper Jumble) when Connor Coyne ran up to me and threw down his tray. He nearly spilled his breakfast on me, grinning like an idiot and saying something about "the reactor."

"What?" I said.

"There's a nuclear reactor on the List!" he said. "There's an article about him—the Nuclear Boy Scout. You have to go look it up! You know how to make a nuclear reactor, right?"

I figured that Connor had slept maybe thirty minutes in the last seventy-two hours, and it was only Thursday morning. His tone bounced somewhere between desperate and manic. I explained that a nuclear reactor is a complex device, and that the physics involved is too complicated for a Scav Hunt item. He answered that the item was worth, like, infinity points and that if we (Justin and I) built something, Mathews would totally win. Back then, Mathews House was its own team, and all forty-five or so of us faced the barbarian hordes alone. I told Connor that I would look into it, but I still didn't believe that there could be something as insane as a nuclear reactor on the List. I mean, really, how irresponsible were the Judges, and how lame were the "reactors" that other teams put together going to be?

After work I stopped at the library and found an article in *Harper's* about David Hahn, "the Nuclear Boy Scout," who had built a modest but plausibly functioning nuclear reactor in a shed in his backyard. Much has been written about David (RIP) in the intervening twenty-plus years, but in the end he did accomplish something in his garden shed. He had assembled a neutron source of some impressive strength for a total amateur, and when unleashed, it met the loosest definition of a nuclear reactor one can imagine. Then the Environmental Protection Agency got involved— but that's another story. An idea was seeded in my brain. On the way home, I ran into Geoff Fischer, a friend and a Judge. No hello or anything. "Are you guys really going to build a nuclear reactor?" he asked. The rumor mill was already in full swing.

I told him I'd need a little clarification on what they meant by "nuclear reactor," and Geoff put me on the phone with Tom Howe, the Head Judge. "A net-power-positive nuclear reactor that could power a city or even a hair dryer is incredibly dangerous and insane," I told Tom. "It's certainly not in the spirit of the item." Item 240 said that the Judges would give credit where Boy Scout credit was due. It clearly referenced Hahn's experiment and not the type of multimegawatt fuel-recycling reactor that Connor and Geoff seemed to be envisioning.

The breeder cycle, for those of you who don't know, creates a larger amount of fissionable fuel material than it uses. By recycling this product, it is able to efficiently generate a large amount of nuclear power, which is why these reactors were popular in the first place. "We can demonstrate the breeder cycle," I told Tom. "We can turn thorium into uranium and uranium into plutonium."

"That's all we want," said Tom, "but we'll have experts there to make sure you're not jerking us around. So be prepared." And he hung up.

By now it was Thursday night. J came home from work and we talked about the idea over a few beers. We agreed that we could use a simple, highly active alpha source to create a weak neutron howitzer that could, in turn, create thermal neutrons. Just like what we used in our physics lab experiments. From there we could make small quantities of whatever isotopes we wanted.

With thorium, it's only a double capture up to uranium[1] with a big cross section.

From there it's another capture up to plutonium, but whatever. We had all weekend, man.

All we needed was a proportional tube and a pulse height analyzer, a NIM crate with preamps and high-voltage power supply, and a few check sources to do a rock-solid calibration. I already had a good alpha source (a few microcuries of radium from World War II–surplus aircraft gauges)

---

1. Thorium (atomic number 90) has ninety protons in the nucleus. Transmuting an atom of thorium into uranium (atomic number 92) requires adding two protons. This is accomplished by bombarding a sample of thorium with slow neutrons from a device called a neutron gun. These neutrons can interact with the thorium nucleus and become "captured" there. After a single successful "capture," the atom of thorium becomes a "heavy" isotope, 233^{Th}. This isotope quickly decays into an isotope of protactinium (atomic number 91). A similar capture and decay process brings the atomic number to 92: uranium.

and thorium dioxide (from the inside of junk vacuum tubes from old TVs that we had salvaged). All we really needed was analytical equipment to verify that it all worked.

The next day, Justin and I visited our favorite lab coordinator, Van Bistro, and asked him ever so nicely if we could borrow a pulse height analyzer, proportional tube, and all the other stuff we needed "for an experiment." Plausible deniability in full effect, Van even loaned us some check sources so we could do an appropriate calibration. All told, we probably signed out on the order of $20,000 worth of highly sensitive equipment. Van basically told us that if anyone so much as sniffed in his direction, he'd claim it was all stolen. And that he had photos of the thieves. We thanked him and carted the junk off to our dorm room.

That night, Justin and I went out to Fermilab to pick up some radiation bunny suits before disappearing into the machine shop. We soldered together some pieces of scrap metal to make an appropriate holder for the radium and thermalizing carbon sheets. It was mostly built of aluminum scrap pieces, but you know—even a boring piece of aluminum I-beam looks impressive with a bit of ingenuity and some face milling. We assembled the main reactor around eight or nine on Saturday night.

By midnight we had finished the energy calibration of the detector. Since our neutron source (the thing driving the nuclear reactions) was laughably weak, we needed to be able to detect down to a single atom whether or not we had indeed created the reactions associated with a breeder reaction. This is where the $20,000 worth of sensitive equipment and our calibrations came into play. By two or three in the morning we had detected the characteristic radiation from neutron capture of thorium, and from there we knew that it was just a waiting game.

At six in the morning we had a solid 3-sigma signal (>

99.7 percent likelihood) demonstrating the production of 235^U. You may have heard of 235^U as "weapons-grade uranium." That's right. We had created the highly fissile isotope of uranium from garbage found under our dorm room workbench. It was an amazing, Promethean moment. We ran down the hallway screaming "We did it! We made uranium!" at the top of our lungs—but this was the Sunday morning of Scav Hunt. Nobody was asleep. As the sun came up on Judgment Day, J and I acquired the same statistical evidence for the production of 239^{Pu}. Weapons-grade plutonium.

Mind you, this might all sound scary, but we detected something like 8,000 individual atoms of uranium, and 2,000 atoms of plutonium, or something like 1×10-18 grams, or way, way less than can be detected by typical chemical tests. This is below the threshold of what might be considered detectable, even in good lab conditions. Our experiment detected the radiation emitted when these elements are created instead of detecting them directly. To detect them directly, given the mind-bogglingly small quantities, would have required a considerable investment of time and effort— two things scarce on Scav Hunt budgets.

Realizing that we would need to show the results to the Judges at some point, we decided to jot down some numbers and essentially write up the experiment like we would in any undergrad physics lab. At 8:45 a.m. Tom called to say that he was at the front desk of the dorm and that he had brought some guests. Next thing we knew, our hallway was filled with four Judges and a jovial but somewhat skeptical guy in his forties. He identified himself as a nuclear engineer from the Kansas City nuclear reactor facility, and he would be passing judgment on our apparatus.

We all piled into Justin's room, some of us tripping over the empty cans. Clothes lay strewn everywhere, over and under crumpled beer cans, and piles of cigarette butts and physics textbooks littered the floor. The nuclear engineer, doubtless accustomed to hyper-clean safety gear and class-10-plus cleanrooms, was less than impressed.

But then Justin and I went into full-on thesis defense mode. J presented some numbers on the capture cross sections and explained the entire capture-decay-capture chain, and I showed him our equipment and explained the design of the reactor and the energy calibration that proved the system's functionality. Five minutes into our argument, the engineer's look turned from mild amusement into complete shell shock. After ten minutes, he had a grin on his face. He wanted to hear all the details of the capture cross sections and the energy calibration. Needless to say, he vouched for us with Tom and the other Judges.

Tom told us to show up at Judgment with our apparatus and a shed to get the points. We piled the reactor in my car and headed over. We threw up a six-cubic-foot drywall shed and spent the rest of the day in radiation suits, dancing to techno music. We kept a cooler in the shed for VIPs. Included among them was a writer covering the Hunt for the AP Wire and another for the *New York Times*. The AP guy seemed afraid of us and, frankly, more interested in the keg toss. The *New York Times* guy, on the other hand, was happy to share our bottle of Veuve Clicquot, as was the winner of *College Jeopardy!* from that year.

Mathews House placed second in the Hunt that year, which was quite an accomplishment for a team of that size. The reactor and all of its baby isotopes were disposed of in accordance with all applicable regulations the following week. A few days later, the editor-in-chief of *Scientific American* contacted us but eventually decided that it wasn't a good idea to publish detailed plans for the production of isotopes in an internationally known magazine, no matter how safe the experiment.

The fallout on campus was pretty mild, all told, although the Resident Heads of the neighboring house evidently asked college housing for our expulsion. Fortunately, the head of housing was familiar with our escapades. As far as I know, any university-level complaints ended at her desk. J and I defended ourselves on several online bulletin boards and communities for the first several months, and then the whole thing more or less faded from the zeitgeist. But the nuclear reactor lives on as a Scav Hunt legend, the prime example of just how far Scavvies will go.

◇◇

Fred Niell graduated from U of C in 1999 with a degree in physics. He lived all four years in Mathews House and Scavved for that team in 1996 and 1997. After Mathews House's dismal outing in 1997, Niell took a year off from Scav in 1998 (save for a spud gun and small item support). Niell went on to graduate school at the University of Michigan and then a string of start-up companies in Boston. He now runs an electrical engineering design consulting company in Tampa, Florida, specializing in high-power and pulsed applications.

FOR EVERY BREEDER REACTOR-TYPE STORY ABOUT

a potentially dangerous or illegal item that goes off without a hitch, there are ten stories about items that could have gone just fine but somehow turned into absurd debacles.

For example, take item 49 of 2005: "A penny smasher that imprints your team logo onto legal tender coins." Sounds charming, right? And maybe for some teams, it was. But for *my* team, the guy trying to imprint the image of an armadillo on to a coin ended up smashing his thumb with a sledgehammer at Judgment. You'd think when blood started pouring out of his hand, that would have stopped him, but you would be underestimating Scavvies. My teammate kept hammering away, trying to make that darn armadillo appear, and then the hammer slipped on the blood and he smashed his thumb *again*. And he *still* tried to keep going, until he was physically stopped and taken to the emergency room. Even then, there were one or two Judges muttering, "I don't know if we should give him full points . . . I can't really see an armadillo on this penny because it's all coated in blood."

In what world is a penny smasher more destructive than a nuclear reactor? In Scav Hunt, apparently.

Every year, Scav's staff advisor reviews the List before it goes out, and she cuts any items that strike her as too dangerous, too destructive, or too illegal. Unfortunately, sometimes you don't find out what the truly destructive items are until it's too late.

ITEM 289:

THE T-SHIRT CANNON

Jake Eberts
2015 SCAV HUNT

289. Fire a T-shirt cannon! Must be a historical T-shirt cannon (made before the Hunt). Please don't shoot any T-shirts that don't have it coming. [6 points; 15 if you fire your team shirt; 25 if you bring it to Judgment for the Judge to fire]

Did it just—it did. Oh my God.

It broke. He broke it.

"What do we do?"

"I'll call the captains."

"You're an idiot, Darren."

Four first years—Anna, Darren, Sarah, and I—from the prestigious University of Chicago stared blankly at the T-shirt cannon in the surprisingly well-maintained basement of a softball stadium somewhere in the northern suburbs of Chicago. The sounds of the crowd yelling outside nicely accentuated the pounding of my heartbeat as I stared at the T-shirt cannon, whose PVC barrel had snapped clean in half.

A quick Google search and call to the captains revealed to us that no, we did not have the money to buy a new one, and no, the captains were not going to magically deliver us from the situation we had gotten ourselves into.

Half an hour ago, we had waltzed into the box office right in the middle of a softball game, demanding access to the stadium's resident T-shirt cannon as if it was our God-given right. Our captains had called ahead, after all. Or someone did, I'm told. The good denizens of the softball stadium had not gotten the memo, apparently, so I heavily name-dropped the university and the Scavenger Hunt, trying to make my explanation of item 289 sound as minimally asinine as I could. I did not drive all the way from Hyde Park to be turned away.

Eventually, someone bought it. We were in. Their mistake.

We were there to launch the BJ Scav team T-shirt as far as we could, and we pursued that goal like it was 1453 and only the walls of Constantinople were stopping us from spreading Islam across a better chunk of the Balkans. We entered the locker room and were struck by the presence of a singular glorified leaf blower with some sick modifications, bathed in the fluorescent light of the locker room's adjacent administrative office. Think Excalibur, but with a Home Depot aesthetic. She was beautiful.

We unsheathed her from her weird holding thing and brought her outside with our team T-shirt in hand. Anna had the honor of firing the device, which we videotaped on my iPhone for Judgment the next day.

But it was a flaccid launch. We had not driven all the way from Hyde Park for any flaccidity. The cannon needed to be charged.

We found the charger in a back closet after asking a confused but helpful stadium worker. The low-energy cannon was going to take a little while to rejuvenate itself, so Darren leaned it against the wall.

That was when the wretched inverse handheld vacuum cleaner tipped over and snapped in half. Oops. Sarah and I made the executive decision to drive to the nearest hardware store, where we spent upward of $30 on various glues and resins and adhesives. Meanwhile, Darren and Anna—

definitely the more anxious half of our troupe to begin with—regularly texted various emoji to me to convey their unease while standing guard over the ravaged body of the cannon. When Sarah and I returned, we all transplanted the corpse back to the locker room proper and made one of the benches our operating table.

I did not drive to the Far North Side from Hyde Park just to nearly pass out from fume inhalation as I smeared various sticky chemicals onto the barrel of this lackluster T-shirt cannon. But that is what happened. Sometimes life does you like that.

The cannon was not a regular piece of equipment in the conventional sense, and neither was it regular in the geometric sense; in other words, we had to hold it upright while the unholy concoction of glue and epoxy resin set because it could not be left in any way so as to allow the barrel to rest on its own. We stood over it and anxiously watched the door. Nobody had come through the locker room yet, but the game had to end at some point, right? Periodically, one of us would cough or twitch and we would have to start over. After several pathetic attempts, the barrel did finally set. We picked it up and moved it around. It fell off after about thirty seconds, which was just peachy.

Up until that point I had done a good job of not letting the miniature cupcakes sitting on a certain Debra's desk in the administrative office tempt me, but I was damn near breaking. We had already bumbled through here and ruined everything like the entitled millennials we were; could eating someone else's cupcakes even make it worse at this point? (I am proud to report that my companions kept me from this, even in my darkest hour.)

Sarah lived in the area and her dad had a workshop—maybe we could transport it back to her house and try to go from there? No, that's a terrible idea. Fine. I give up. After about two hours, I yanked a piece of printer paper from Debra's desk and took one of her nice pens and wrote in flowing, elegant script:

Hi! We are the University of Chicago students who came in to borrow your T-shirt cannon. Thank you so much for letting us use it! Unfortunately, it got bumped a little and the barrel seems to have broken. We tried to fix it ourselves but haven't been lucky so far and are on a tight schedule. If you can't fix it easily and need it replaced, I'll leave my cell number so we can figure it out. Sorry again about the accident!

I emailed our final product—"the very underwhelming and very stressful T-shirt launch that ultimately taught us a lot about friendship, teamwork and how useless rubber cement is.MOV"—to a Lieutenant Kathryn (think page captains but more entitled), and it earned us 15 delicious points worth every skipped heartbeat the day before had entailed.

For a full month afterward, I fended off panic attacks every time my phone buzzed. But no one ever called, so my friends and I choose to believe everything worked out fine. Part of me sort of hoped that someone would call and berate us for our blatant disregard for the property of others, but the thing about Scav Hunt is that sometimes you get away with a lot more than you should.

Jake Eberts is a political science major from the Class of 2019. He began Scavving for his dorm, Burton-Judson, his first year and continued to do so the following year as a lieutenant, and then again as a BJ captain in 2017.

MANY SCAVVIES HAVE BEEN IN SITUATIONS LIKE THE one Jake Eberts describes in the previous essay, where they demand help from outsiders "as if it was our God-given right." It's uncomfortable but important for Scavvies to remind themselves that (a) it's *not* our God-given right, and (b) not everyone has the privilege to behave in this way.

I remember one Scav throwing on a dress at the H&M downtown and racing to the front of the store to pose in the window for a photograph. (The item was "Mannequin, or mannic*an't*?") An employee tried to stop me. "You're not allowed to wear that out of the dressing room," he told me.

"It's for a *scavenger hunt*," I explained, in that moment fully confident that this gave me all the reason I needed to break the rules.

"I'll get in trouble," he told me.

And I care *now*—this memory digs into my conscience and shames me now, that I would have so little concern for a stranger's job if it stood between me and Scav—but as it was happening, I didn't care about anything except completing the item.

Scav Hunt gives you so many accomplishments to feel proud of. And sometimes, it gives you things to feel really rotten about, too.

ITEM 159:

DADDY ISSUES

Jennifer Joos

1994 SCAV HUNT

My father was not blinded in a carpentry accident, and I feel guilty about that. I'm not a bad person, I don't think, but I've told some lies in my life. However, none of them compare to the grisly falsehood I wove for the Snell-Hitchcock team during the 1994 Hunt.

159. A Braille Playboy. [83 points]

I could tell this item was going to be difficult because it had a high point value. But I had been doing Scav Hunt since 1992, I had obtained many exotic (and on one occasion illegal) items, and I was up for the challenge. I was determined to get a braille *Playboy*. I would not let my teammates down.

I first tried calling the Chicago Public Library. Unfortunately, the library had already loaned its braille *Playboy* to a competitor who had called before me. Strike one.

I did manage to cadge from the librarian the phone number of a Chicago-based service that converted magazines into braille. If you can't find one, make one, I thought. A fine idea . . . except the braille service would take weeks to fill a single order. I had four days. Strike two.

Desperate, I dialed *Playboy*'s Chicago office. "I'm looking for a braille *Playboy*," I told three confused operators before being connected to a woman who, upon hearing my request, sighed loudly.

"Is this for that scavenger hunt thing?" she asked.

I didn't even pause. "Excuse me?" I huffed.

"Are you calling about a braille *Playboy* for the Scavenger Hunt? Because I'm getting really tired of these calls."

That's when I started to cry. Loud, snot-filled sobs shook my whole body. I startled myself, but, more importantly, I startled the *Playboy* secretary on the other end of the line. The dark, twisted part of my brain took over, and out came this unrehearsed story:

My father had recently been blinded in a carpentry accident. He was now in rehabilitation and struggling to learn braille. It was difficult for him, but he refused to give up and kept his spirits high by trying to make light of his situation. The joke he told everyone who visited him in the hospital was that the thing he would miss most about losing his sight was seeing his monthly copy of *Playboy*.

My dad's fiftieth birthday was coming up and I wanted to give him a gift that would not only encourage him as he worked to learn braille, but would also keep him in touch with his old life. I needed a braille *Playboy*. And considering all my family had been through recently, I certainly did not appreciate being met with an insensitive attitude or accusations of being on a scavenger hunt.

This was not the first time I had invented a father. In fact, I fictitiously create and then kill off family members at the drop of a hat. I was born to unwed teenage parents. My dad disappeared into the ether when I was about two years old. Just vanished. I suppose my mom could have tracked him down, but she didn't and I grew up feeling like my father was a taboo topic. I never asked about him and know nothing about him except his name. I certainly didn't know when his fiftieth birthday was. Then I emancipated myself from my mother when I matriculated at U of C. My invented blind carpenter father was as real a parent as I had.

When I concluded my story, the secretary shakily asked me to hold. Meanwhile, I reasoned with myself that it's always possible my dad really *was* a blind *Playboy* subscriber. How would I know? When the *Playboy* employee came back on the line, she rewarded my lie with heartfelt sympathy and a guarantee of as many braille *Playboys* as I wanted.

The only snag was that my need was time-sensitive. The Scavenger Hunt deadline, masquerading as my blind father's fiftieth birthday, was Sunday. It was already Friday.

It turns out that braille *Playboys* are made to fulfill subscriptions, so there aren't just piles of them lying around the Chicago office. My *Playboy* contact scrambled to help. She put me on hold and called their printing warehouse somewhere in the Southeast. She kept checking back in with me as she dispatched employees throughout the warehouse in search of an issue that may have been overlooked. After half an hour, a lone box containing an old issue had been found.

The secretary now asked me where they should send the magazine. I had not planned for this. I had not planned for anything, I suppose, but I gritted my teeth and gave her the address of my dorm, omitting the "Snell-Hitchcock" part. I altered my room number to an apartment number. I hoped she wouldn't match up the 57th Street address with the University of Chicago and draw the logical conclusion that I was indeed doing this for the Scavenger Hunt and not for my poor, blind dad.

She did not. Instead, she wished me well and on behalf of *Playboy* thanked my father for his readership, which she delicately said she hoped would continue.

Home run. I left my dorm room flushed and shaking, my body coursing with adrenaline. I was triumphant when I announced to the team what I had done. Triumphant and nauseated. My teammates all said how proud of me they were, while I tried to feel proud of myself.

The next morning I received a call from the dorm's front desk attendant: there was a delivery waiting for me. I ran to find an enormous box. FedEx overnight, Saturday delivery—this was probably a very pricey package to send, yet I was holding it and it was free and it was filled with braille *Playboys*.

Braille *Playboys* are big, about seventeen by twelve inches. It takes three braille volumes to reproduce a single conventional issue. They are constructed from thick, creamy beige paper. The only visible print is on the cover: issue number, date, the name *Playboy* spelled out, and the iconic bunny logo in black.

I ran my fingers over bumps that were incomprehensible to me, though they would have been understood by my blind father, perhaps. The magazines were so spare and minimal. They were beautiful. Really, they were art objects worthy of display. I toyed with the idea of framing them or putting them under glass in the future, when Scav Hunt was over, when I was a full-fledged adult with a home.

We won that year. Snell-Hitchcock got its ice cream social, complete with a giant, plastic, pillow-like bag of non-dairy whipped topping. Of course there were hundreds of items on the List, so it's not as if my braille *Playboy* single-handedly won the Hunt for us . . . but it certainly helped. On Sunday night, other objects were disposed of, dismantled, and returned, but the braille *Playboys* stayed with me.

Though I have been an adult with a home for many years now, I never put the magazines on display, as I had originally imagined. I never showed them to anyone at all. They haunted me. Good people with decent, loving families would never invent such a horrible lie. Good people don't swindle nice women over the telephone. I had been good at Scav Hunt. I had not been a good person. I don't know if that was a fair trade-off.

Still, I felt the magazines said something important about me, like the embarrassing junior high school journal you hold on to, even though you never want to remember junior high. So I kept the Playboys after graduation and through several moves across the country: Chicago to Montana to Washington to Maine.

In 2007, I was packing up my house for yet another move, this time from Maine to Alabama. As I had so many times in the past thirteen years, I came across the braille Playboys in the bottom of a box. I felt the familiar feeling of triumph when I thought about Snell-Hitchcock's 1994 Scav Hunt win, as well as that familiar sense of guilt. I decided then that it was time to let them go.

I've found it better, in my life, to put things that sadden or shame me out of my mind. This is most easily accomplished when there is no physical trace of those things. I never had any photographs of my real father, and I never wanted any. I didn't want the braille Playboys any more, either. I threw the oversized volumes in the trash. They're decomposing in a Maine landfill where they don't define my goodness, and I have a little more peace in my life.

Jennifer Joos graduated from the University of Chicago in 1995 with a BA in English language and literature. She competed for the Snell-Hitchcock Scavenger Hunt team from 1992 to 1995. Jennifer currently resides in Auburn, AL, where she is a prospect researcher at Auburn University, working to identify new donors to build a university performing arts center.

JENNIFER JOOS'S APPROACH TO SECURING A BRAILLE

Playboy and Jake Eberts's approach to securing a T-shirt cannon may be considered somewhat *immoral*, but they're not *illegal*, which is where we really draw the line. The very first rule on the List every year is this:

"All items on the List can be obtained and performed legally. It may involve smooth talking, or it may involve something else, but it is all possible."

All items can be obtained legally; however, that's not always the route that the Scavvies choose to take.

6 ITEMS THAT MAYBE
WEREN'T 100 PERCENT LEGAL

1988.76: An Indiana Bell manhole cover (there are extras you know!)
[25 points]

> Scav lore has it that, years later, Scav founder (and
> radiologist) Christopher Straus had the chief of
> the Gary, Indiana, police force as a patient. Making
> small talk, Dr. Straus asked the chief about the
> weirdest cases he had encountered, and the man in-
> formed him of this one weekend in the late eighties
> when all the manhole covers in town disappeared
> for some reason. At which point, Dr. Straus kept his
> mouth shut.

1989.142: A real telephone pole (It's easier to move without the wires!)
[150 points]

> The Judges knew that decommissioned telephone
> poles could be found in many electrical yards across
> the city of Chicago. Unfortunately, there were also
> apartments being built at 55th and Blackstone at
> the time of the Hunt, with a removed telephone
> pole lying on the ground, which was not actually up
> for the taking. The Hitchcock team brought a little
> dolly to the pole, but, stealth not being part of their
> capabilities, they were quickly caught by a UCPD
> officer and forced to return it. The Breckinridge
> team tried to nab the pole next, so the thwarted

Hitchcock captain called the UCPD himself. And so, for the remainder of the weekend, the UCPD's first "24 Hour Pole Watch" was put in place.

1990.284: A full sized authentic "L" car used by the C.T.A. [1,000 points]

An item that was almost completed (as in, the CTA was willing and ready for transport) until the Chicago Department of Transportation nixed it for fear that the weight of the car would collapse the roads around Ida Noyes.

1997.019: A webpage your team has written explaining your cult—points awarded for complexity, oddness, and coolness (and not how long it takes to load); must include the Hale-Bopp comet, the RAS, and Bjork, as well as other links you think the judges may enjoy; URLs must be sent to Mike Campion via e-mail, at [REDACTED], by Saturday, May 3, 1997, 10pm [40 points]

Two members of the Shoreland team were trying to gain an advantage by tracking the actions of the *Maroon*/MUNUC/Blackstone Coalition HOPE team. Late at night, they cracked the password of a member of the *Maroon* staff, gaining access to HOPE's website. The owner of the account was also a very close observer of the login logs and was extremely unhappy with the unauthorized login. He complained to the Judges, who, following a hard interpretation of the "don't interfere with other teams' items" rule (and hoping to head off future cybersabotage), disqualified the Shoreland team, giving the 1997 Hunt victory to Snell-Hitchcock.

2005.08: How fucking strong are you, bitch? Can you fucking toss a refrigerator, bitch? How fucking far can you fucking throw it? Then fucking do it. Please. BYOFR (bitch)

> One of the few items cut mid-hunt by Office of the Reynolds Club and Student Activities (ORCSA) due to sudden concerns about Freon leakage.

2006.296: How many UofC students does it take to change a light bulb? What if that light bulb is at 919 N. Michigan Ave? [1 point]

> A reference to the rotating "Lindbergh Beacon" atop the Palmolive building, used for several decades to guide airplanes to Midway Airport. It was shut off in 1981 due to complaints from residents of nearby buildings. By 2006, it was only occasionally lit; however, as several U of C students found out that year, the doors to it were left unlocked. But if you go through those doors and start taking pictures, eventually a nice security guard will arrive, believing you're about to do some terrorism. Let's just say it was an interesting phone call.

SOME OF THE MOST MEMORABLE SCAV EXPERIENCES come from times when Scavvies encounter normal people, strangers from outside of the U of C, folks who are just going about their day and have no frame of reference for the point-crazed maniacs coming at them. For example, for item 131 in 2004, I joined a horde of Scavvies dressed as Care Bears who went downtown to a goth convention to introduce some goth youths to sunshine and lollipops. Here's how the goths felt about having their convention interrupted by our Care Bear cosplay: *not great*. But for us, the juxtaposition was hilarious, and the points were more than worth it.

Sometimes Scav crosses paths with goths, and other times it's with the Chicago Transit Authority, secretaries at *Playboy*, softball field administrators named Debra, or, hell, even the world's foremost primatologist, Jane Goodall. When doing Scav, you just never know whom you might meet.

ITEM 161:

CULTURE SHOCK

Joel Putnam
2010 SCAV HUNT

Inside Rockefeller Chapel, around 10 p.m. on Friday, May 7, renowned scientist Jane Goodall had just finished giving a speech. She had moved to the enclosed front vestibule of the church, where the atmosphere was quiet and respectful. Ms. Goodall, seated with her back to the church's large outer front doors, patiently autographed books and smiled for photographs. She was there for each and every one of her admirers who had attended, who were being let in through the inner doors she faced at a controlled trickle. On the other side of these doors, beneath the vaulted neo-Gothic ceiling, was a throng of giddy fans waiting for Goodall. They were lined up from the front entrance all the way back up to the altar.

Past them was a small group that looked a little out of place. For one thing, they were all wearing tuxedo-print T-shirts with green tentacles printed on the front and back. For another, they weren't that excited about Jane Goodall. They looked nervous.

I was one of these people.

My friend Daniel, also in a tux T-shirt, came up to us. "Go out to the front," he said.

We stared at him. And all started talking at once.

"What's there?"

"*Who's* there?"

"Do you mean they—"

"But it's not 10:30 yet!"

"Just go and look!"

I darted for a side door out of the chapel, flanked and followed by my colleagues. We dodged pews, hit the side doors, banked left, and ran past the lit-from-the-bottom stone wall of the church. We skidded to a halt at the lawn outside the grand front entrance and stared.

Roughly a hundred people were limping their way toward us, groaning and occasionally screaming. Their clothing was dirty rags, their faces were covered in blood and boils, and a few of them were missing limbs and chunks of flesh. The seething mass was inching closer to the heavy front doors of the church. The doors with Jane Goodall and several hundred fans sitting sedately and reverently on the other side.

This wasn't a zombie attack. This was a scheduling conflict. The world-famous primatologist and UN Messenger of Peace had simply had the bad fortune of being scheduled at the same time as the following Scav item:

161. May 7, 2010, 10:30 pm. A foul wind tosses decayed leaves in my face with almost willful malevolence as I trudge toward the Chapel. Its soaring belltower, once proud, now seems craven, afraid of the unhallowed Mass it will soon host. The sagging gambrel roofs of the campus architectures likewise cower as we approach, their weathered walls and ruined faces a mockery of the pustules and pockmarks that cover my companions. Shunned by the campus, denied by the hospitals, we march onward, determined to revel in our grisly condition. Our masks may do little to conceal our Afflictions, but in a fit of gallows humour we have decorated them gaily, and will throw a Masque in our dying hours. Each family has appointed its most wretched specimen a Seed of Corruption, whom we venerate with savage glee; their twisted countenances defy description by even a madman such as myself. When the clock strikes midnight I expect we shall all be dead, but until then we shall dance as though to tire Death himself. [ω points]

So, we had a mass of university students and alumni in costumes inspired by nine or ten awful diseases (plus one team inexplicably dressed in *World of Warcraft* outfits), descending on Jane Goodall and her fans.

I hadn't expected this either. Yes, I was a Judge. But I was an emeritus Judge. I'd graduated two years prior and was just coming back to visit. In fact, I'd been out of the country for over a year and a half, backpacking through sixty-something countries across all seven continents. I'd been spending my days salsa dancing at Mexican street parties, winning poker games on the Trans-Siberian Railway, and zip-lining off the Great Wall of China. I'd returned to the US just a week before, stopping by Chicago just in time for Scav.

Using the full power bestowed on us as Judges—and some of our loudest yelling—we held the disease-riddled mass at bay long enough for Goodall and company to wrap up. As far as I am aware, Jane Goodall never knew that she was very nearly the victim of a zombie incursion. And then we opened the floodgates and let the zombie party start in the perfect gothic setting.

If I had to return to regular life, this wasn't a bad way to do it.

When the people I met on my trip learned that I was traveling around the world, they would sometimes ask me to talk about my weirdest cultural experiences. But even though I'd been to some pretty exotic places, I often had a hard time coming up with a good answer. It wasn't until four hours after the midnight List Release, when Judge headquarters received its fourth or fifth delivery from Scav teams of a fully cooked ham, bone-in, that I started thinking maybe it's because, sometimes, the weirdest place in the world is right at home. As the hams piled up in the refrigerator, on the countertops, and in the hallway in the wee hours of the morning, I realized that it's hard to think of any place in this world I could honestly call normal.

36. Gimme gimme gimme a ham after midnight. But before sunrise on Thursday. Piping hot, freshly baked, fully glazed, bone-in. Deliver to [REDACTED] S. Harper Ave. [40 points]

Joel Putnam graduated from the College in 2008 with a double major in political science and international studies. Prior to becoming a Judge in fall 2007, he Scavved for Pierce and later MacPierce. He is currently the interim director for the Focus Forward Project, a criminal justice nonprofit in New York City. You can read more about his adventures at joelrputnam.com.

BECOMING A SCAV HUNT JUDGE IS AN INVOLVED PRO- cess, but once you've done it, you're in for life, which is why Joel Putnam could show up after a year and a half of exploring the world, throw on a T-shirt that said "JUDGE," and be right at home.

In the first years of Scav, as Diane Kelly described earlier, you got to be a Judge pretty much just by having Judge friends. But by the time I applied for the Judgeship, in the fall of 2005, the application process was much more formalized and required submitting a list of thirty sample items, explaining why I would or would not support various fictional items, sitting for an interview, and more. The existing Judges consider all the applications and select a handful of new members to add to their ranks.

For the next six months, the Judges meet for hours every week. First they brainstorm and workshop potential items, individually and in small groups before taking them before the Judgeship as a whole. Each item is passed or rejected through a simple thumbs-up, thumbs-down vote, with the majority ruling. A Judge can argue vehemently for his or her proposed items, but if you can't convince the majority of the group, it won't make it on to the List.

Next the Judges work out the wording for the items, to make them appropriately clever and hard to parse. They cut any items that are too similar to one another, including items that are repeats of ones on past years' Lists. They point the List, deciding on the maximum possible value of each item. They run the whole thing past a staff advisor, who tries to figure out what the items mean well enough so that she can cut anything that seems destined for a lawsuit. They figure out the schedule of events, reserve the necessary spaces and supplies, and, during the four days of the Hunt itself, generally sleep under one roof in whichever Judge's apartment is the biggest (and whose roommates didn't refuse).

Needless to say, the Judges spend a *lot* of time together.

Unsurprisingly, out of all that togetherness and all that institutional history come inside jokes. And those jokes grow in complexity year after year. As with any group culture, there's no predicting what will become an inside joke with staying power. For the Judges, for example, coleslaw became one such joke.

11 ITEMS WHOSE ANSWER WAS "COLESLAW"

2005.139: What's an acrostic? [1 point. 3 bonus points]

> One of Scav's enduring recent traditions is the Judg-
> es' tendency to request coleslaw in various obfus-
> cated ways. Like many Scav traditions, serendipity
> had a role to play in its creation. You see, the idea
> was that Scavvies, hinted by this item's reference to
> acrostics, would notice that the first letter of each
> of the items on the page where it appeared (page
> 8, incidentally) spelled out "BRING ME COLESLAW."
> Since this item was set to be the last of fifteen on
> the page, the item required had to fit in the span
> of fifteen letters and end with a W. Once the Judges
> remembered how much they loved coleslaw, things
> fell into place rather quickly.

2006.28: 5714 1 SCAV DRUOKLLZFRWPYRIFDTX. [6 points]

> Run this string of letters with the given settings
> through a World War II-era Enigma machine (or at
> least the machine at the Museum of Science and
> Industry, close to the U of C campus), and you'll get
> "BRINGEN MIR KRAUTSALAT," "krautsalat," natural-
> ly, being the German word for coleslaw. No team
> had gotten the item in 2005, so it was thought that
> repeating the joke would be hilarious. And it was,
> especially since, again, no team was able to crack

the code: the Max Palevsky team came close, though
they received no points for their sauerkraut.

2007.190: 35°40'N 139°45'E, 41°45'N 72°40'W, 55°56'N 3°11'W,
22°33'N 88°22'E, 21°0'N 105°51'E, 63°45'N 68°31'W, 40°50'N
115°46'W, 50°6'N 8°42'E, 25°44'S 28°12'E, 32°57'S 60°40'W,
34°41'N 135°31'E, 53°20'N 6°15'W, 59°51'N 17°38'E, 41°52'N
87°41'W, 41°39'N 83°32'W, 47°16'N 11°24'E, 40°46'N 73°58'W,
35°42'N 51°29'E, 52°23'N 9°43'E, 36°7'S 144°45'E, 32°23'N
62°6'E, 22°54'S 43°14'W, 2°55'N 11°9'E, 40°46'N 111°53'W,
53°35'N 10°1'E, 51°43'N 75°19'E, 32°6'N 114°4'E, 48°50'N 2°20'E,
41°53'N 12°29'E, 53°34'N 113°31'W, 23°32'S 46°37'W, 32°42'N
117°9'W, 33°51'S 151°12'E, 40°44'N 89°36'W, 11°20'N 162°20'E,
50°56'N 6°57'E, 39°46'N 86°9'W, 25°16'S 57°40'W, 38°14'N
85°44'W, 37°15'S 12°30'W, 28°46'N 104°37'E, 53°47'N 1°32'W,
38°55'N 1°26'E, 40°53'N 73°20'W, 40°52'N 73°18'W. [3 points]

These forty-five pairs of latitudes and longitudes
point to forty-five major cities (many of which
feature a Scav Hunt connection). Taking the first
letter of each of these cities gives you THE CHIEF
PRODUCT IN THE FRESH EXPRESS SPECIALTY LINE.
This was the first time teams managed to provide
coleslaw when asked. But, if you do something three
times in Scav Hunt, well, it's a tradition!

2008.214: 22818877@N06 and 2008.119: Execute The Plan! [38
points]

With Scavvies becoming wise to coleslaw's increas-
ing prominence on the list, the natural Judge-
Scavvie arms race led to the references becoming
increasingly esoteric. This year's List included
multiple puzzle items, only one of which requested
coleslaw. Present coleslaw at the wrong time, and

you'll receive no points. This item is a reference to a Flickr account that would send you down the rabbit hole of various puzzles that would eventually reveal that "The Plan" was to fill a sock with coleslaw and slap a judge with it.

2009.207: Bring back the golden age of radio for at least 10 thrilling minutes! We'll give you the time slot at WHPK, you provide script, sound effects, impersonations, wit, humor, and drama. Your broadcast must have an original serialized radio drama, punctuated by an annoying call sign and commercials, no less than once every three minutes. All breaks from the action must leave us on cliff-hangers that compel us not to change that dial. The Judges will provide you an encoded message to broadcast for all "junior judges" to decipher with item 2009.217. Teams must combine decoded messages from all teams' radio broadcasts to figure out the secret instructions. [40 points, 10 points for advertising your serial in the Reynolds Club in the proper '30s style, and 10 points for decoding the message]

Item 2009.217 refers to decoder rings that were passed out at that year's Captains' Breakfast, and the message was: "be sure to eat your coleslaw."

2010.245: 4a3l3n3p2e2ibcdgkorsuw [7 points]

This was inspired by a code in a then-recent installment of *Dinosaur Comics*, in which a secret phrase had all its letters sorted by frequency. So, for example, the phrase "SHAQ'S YOUR MOM" would become "2m2o2sahrquy," since the phrase has two Ms, two Os, two Ss, one A, etc. The Scav version (which became easier to solve if the team realized that this was the coleslaw item) led to "COLESLAW IN A PINK AND PURPLE BAG." Unfortunately, the

South Campus team got only as far as "COLESLAW KIDNAPPING," leading to a judge being randomly abducted with a hood of coleslaw during that year's HQ visit. Whoops.

2011.257: https://www.youtube.com/watch?v=yfOGl8JUowg

This is a now-inactive link to a YouTube video of a Judge performing the dance language of Eurythmy to present the phrase "sweet dreams are made of coleslaw."

2012.12: This item is hidden in a campus building on the Quads. [4 points]

Sprinkled around the interior walls of the buildings on the U of C quads are pieces of an art installation that replicates various academic citations, now accompanied by one impressive bit of fakery supplied by the Judges, citing "Coleslaw, modernity and immigration." Last time we checked, it had not yet been taken down.

2012.122: TACTCAGGATAGTTACGGACAGTAACTTACACCT AGTGGGTAACTTACCTAGCGCTCTCATCATAGTTACCCACTTAC TAGTTAACTTACCGGACTTACAAAGAACGGTCATTTACT [3 prime points]

Teams were meant to (1) recognize this as DNA code, (2) transcribe it to RNA, (3) find the proper tRNA anticodon, then (4) convert to the proper three-letter amino acid. And they did! Properly spaced, the solution was "spinach with dressing in a flask," since neither "cabbage" nor "coleslaw" can be spelled with amino acid sequences.

2014b.171: A foodstuff which you believe best represents H.R. 3263 (112th Congress), the Lake Thunderbird Efficient Use Act of 2012; H.R. 5883 (112th Congress), To designate the facility of the United States Postal Service located at 115 4th Avenue Southwest Ardmore, Oklahoma, as the "Specialist Michael E. Phillips Post Office"; or H.R. 4066 (108th Congress), Chickasaw National Recreation Area Land Exchange Act of 2004. [H.R. 2 points]

> The common factor linking each of these bills is that, at the time of the list, they were the only bills introduced by Rep. Tom Cole (R-OK) that had been signed into federal law. Or, in other words, they are . . . Cole's laws.

2015 Scav Wedding Item 3: Execute the plan! As they exit the chapel, shower the Scavvenbride and Scavvengroom with the Hunt's favorite diced vegetable (hold the mayo . . . that tux is rented!). [3 points]

> Why get showered with the boringly traditional rice as you recess down the aisle, when you could get pelted with coleslaw?

SOMETIMES, AS IN THE CASE OF "COLESLAW KIDNAPPING,"
Scavvies make things harder on themselves than they need to. The next essay is a classic example of that. The author would have gotten the same number of points for his team had he completed this next item in a simpler way . . . but he would have been left with a much more boring story.

ITEM 42:

THE FORBIDDEN FRUIT

David Muraskin

2003 SCAV HUNT

We're in the final leg of the Road Trip, and I may have an awkward problem.

We've driven hundreds of miles through Illinois over the past three days, from Carbondale in the far south up to the northern border with Wisconsin. I'm wearing the same black sweats I started out the weekend in, but thankfully have been able to take off the boxing gloves and *lucha libre* mask cut from an orange beach ball, which had transformed me from awkward Fundamentals: Issues and Texts major (my major has a colon in it, get on board) into Strong Bad of the *Homestar Runner* flash cartoon series.

Yet, now, on this final stretch, as we head toward home and I'm beginning to imagine telling our tales to the team we left behind, I can't help noticing that I itch. Like, down there.

It must be the lack of sleep.

Or maybe the lack of shower.

Yeah, it's probably just sweat, everyone sweats— particularly nineteen-year-old boys who haven't changed their pants in days. This is not. a. big. deal.

I discreetly scratch as we drive around the South Side of Chicago, looking for kids' basketball hoops so we can complete one more item before we call it a day. (Item 34: "Slammin' on one hoop is cool but slammin' on 20 hoops in one place is supa-fly, especially if you're a cartoon.") Certainly we were meant to do this somewhere else (still not sure where), but if there are rules to Scav, the first rule is "something is better than nothing."

By the time we pull up in front of our dorm, it's shortly before dawn on Judgment Day. I spend a couple hours getting the videos of our items in order so we can show them to the Judges. A brief nap, and then I'm back up for Judgment itself, admiring what was created while I was on the road, like a nine-inch pianist (item 54) and a meticulously crafted Foam Chomsky (item 251).

With all of these distractions, it's not until after dinner Sunday night that I notice no shower, change of clothes, or amount of sleep is fixing my itch. And that's when I realize what happened.

41. Turn the Garden of the Gods into the Garden of Eden, replete with Genesis garb. Don't forget to eat the forbidden fruit and to throw yourselves out. [45 points]

It wouldn't have been my first choice to take this on, but I knew it was my turn. My fellow road-trippers had already taken their lumps for the good of the order.

Before we even left campus on Thursday morning, the most senior member of our car had been called to the basement of the Reynolds Club for item 111: "Give IT back to us at the end of the trip [150 points]." IT was a button that the Judges had him swallow in a spoonful of ice cream. There were only two ways to get this button out: through the top, or through the bottom. A runner was sent to get ipecac that kicked in exactly as we were turning onto the Dan Ryan Expressway. I remain thankful that we'd brought a trash can to capture the spew (and the button).

Then another one of my teammates handled the first

nudity item, 229, "A natural bridge means you must take a picture au natural."

So when we got to Shawnee National Forest's Garden of the Gods, I had to step up. I agreed to be videotaped as if in the Garden of Eden, noshing on an apple, while my team members screamed at me to get the hell out.

But how much like I had just been made by my Creator did I need to appear, exactly? I was a nineteen-year-old boy. This was going to be recorded. And that recording was going to be shown in a room full of people, some of whom were going to be nineteen-year-old girls.

We needed to do some critical reading of "Genesis garb." Sure, the paintings always show Eve provocatively hidden behind locks of hair or well-placed branches. The implication is that she and Adam wore no garb at all. But that is an artistic choice, meant to capture the viewer's attention. It is a garden. There *were* branches. Branches *mean* leaves. Leaves *could* be put together for coverings. What do we know about Adam and Eve's sense of modesty and style, really?

Problem solved, in theory.

However, this is May. Leaves on the trees are budding, not covering. So I turned to the ground. It is a national *forest* after all; there has to be some brush, a shrub, grasses, something. And sure enough there was, at the base of a tree right across from where we had set up the scene. Unlike everything else, these were large leaves that appeared to be in almost full bloom. There were so many coming off the center stem that you could just rip a couple of the plants out and be sure of complete coverage in both front and back, leaves not just hiding the key facts but creating a full skirt.

What harm could there be in showing man's dominion over the garden's vegetation, right?

Right.

Until the nurse I see as soon as the student care center

opens on Monday confirms that the brush I had chosen for my Genesis garb was poison oak.

When you have red hives covering your upper thighs, buttocks, and penis, the worry is no longer whether viewers of a camcorder screen will be impressed. All of a sudden it's the much more practical and permanent issue of scarring, in places you don't want to have a scar.

The solution, oral antihistamines, has the nice added side effect of knocking you out so that you don't think about the welts covering your nether regions.

That worked well for a day and a half.

Then Wednesday came.

Wednesday I had my once-a-week class that seemed too big-deal to miss. It was taught by a public intellectual who we were to feel honored had taken the time. We were reading Jean-Jacques Rousseau's *Emile*, a book on how to best educate the children of the Republic.

This public intellectual had made clear if we were to have any chance of understanding the nuances of Rousseau, attending class was essential. You see, he and Rousseau were kindred spirits. We were not merely being guided in reading and analyzing Rousseau; through showing up, we were ourselves receiving the *Emile*'s education.

So I walked in pharmaceutical-free, convinced I would mind-over-matter this shit and prove what the U of C is made of: we Scav on the weekends and attend salons during the week.

I popped my first pill within five minutes of sitting down. Rousseau, even when read out loud in the original French, can't pull your focus away from a testicular itch. Although it may have helped if I, and not just the public intellectual, spoke French.

When the first pill didn't take effect, I took a second.

It came as no real surprise that at the midclass break

the public intellectual called me over to say I needed to leave. He had noticed that I was in no position to appreciate him or the *Emile*. I was half passed out, sliding down in my chair to use the back as a headrest.

I sheepishly tried to explain what had happened. I think I said something like, "I got sick going through some brush in the national forest." This only led the public intellectual to chide me for missing a central principle of the *Emile*: we must be wary when we expose our children to nature. Plainly, this was a good point; I just hadn't realized Rousseau had anticipated the risks of rubbing poison oak over your junk.

So maybe I missed some of the key insights of the *Emile*. But the teachings that stick with me are the ones I learned from Scav. Being part of an *event*, particularly a *big* event, exposes you to the most important lessons, and it certainly is what makes you think beyond yourself and of the Republic. Even if it results in a genital rash, it's worth it. At least, as long as there are oral antihistamines on hand.

David Muraskin graduated from the College in 2005 with concentrations in Fundamentals: Issues and Texts and political science. He participated in Scav all four years as a member of Phoenix Rising (2002), Phoenix Does Dallas (2003), The Emperor's New Outfit (2004), and The Emperor Strikes Back (2005). He is currently a public interest lawyer in Washington, DC, where he focuses on constitutional, consumer, and environmental litigation.

WHILE DAVE MURASKIN WAS OFF ON HIS WAY·TOO·
natural road trip, this next writer was simultaneously on a separate
team, on an ill-fated road trip of his own. Although this Scavvie
encountered no poison oak, he hit his own unnecessary natural
disaster.

ITEM 32:

WE TEMPT THE WRATH OF GOD

Doug Diamond
2003 SCAV HUNT

I shouldn't have said it. I knew I shouldn't have said it. But I've just never been good at keeping my mouth shut.

When I let the fateful words slip, my Road Trip team was in Effingham, Illinois, defiling the monuments of the Ten Commandments that surround a 200-foot crucifix.

32. On four sides of a giant cross there are words. Find out what those words are and take a picture next to the side Homestar'd most like to pee on. [12 points]

Holly, Birge, and I were dressed up as the *Homestar Runner* crew, an internet show that had inspired the Road Trip dress code that year. Holly, fellow exhibitionist and primary navigator, was Homestar and was breaking as many commandments as she could without using her arms. Birge dressed as the Cheat and helped out. I was Strong Bad, though my costume's boxing gloves made it awfully difficult to pee on the Ten Commandments. Joe, our final Road Trip team member and a student of cinema, filmed the whole event.

As we left the crucifix and walked back to the car, we made the requisite jokes about how we were all going to hell, and how God was going to punish us with lightning and a deluge, and how we would never finish the Road Trip, blah-blah-funny-hah. And *that* is when I said it.

"Don't worry." I laughed. "We'll have plenty of time to wreck the car later."

We piled back into the car, me behind the wheel and Holly behind the map, and tore off at breakneck speed. I did most of the driving, as I was willing to speed more excessively than the others. When it came to Scav, I was willing to do *everything* more excessively than others.

It was 2003, my third year as a Scavvie, and I thought we had a pretty damn good Road Trip team. I had jumped ship from the Shoreland that year to go to the FIST, where it wasn't just about winning, even though we really wanted to win. It was about doing cooler and crazier shit than everyone else. We were the most nuts, and we were going to prove it.

So far on that Road Trip we were doing an excellent job of just that. We were knocking off items, we had a distance lead on a lot of the competition, and our antics were serving as inspiration to the rest of the FIST team back on campus. But all this was before we hit Decatur.

The night after we peed on God's rules for humanity, we got a motel room because we needed to recharge the video camera batteries. As long as we were there, we figured we'd shower and catch a few winks.

Unfortunately, the motel floor was so comfortable that we ended up sleeping longer than we had planned. We woke up after six hours, anxious to make up for the lost time. Problem was, there was now a deluge outside.

From our motel room window, we watched the rain pour down in sheets, the kind of storm that windshield wipers have no chance of contending with. We shouldn't have gone out in it. We should have waited it out in our dry, warm motel room. But we had overslept, and we didn't have the time to waste.

A half hour later, we were driving down Water Street
(har-de-har-har, I know), which soon ran under an overpass.
There looked to be about a foot of standing water underneath the overpass. I drove to the edge and stopped.

"Do you think we can make it?" I asked. Almost before
anybody had time to respond (though I still swear that at
least one person said, "Go for it!"), I gunned the engine and
drove straight in.

To understand my decision-making process, you have to
realize that we were in a Subaru. My Subaru. A Subaru that I
had taken off-roading on snowmobile trails, that had forded
streams in Pennsylvania, that had been my constant com-
panion despite 120,000 miles of shameless abuse. I didn't
think of this machine as a car. It was an extension of my
recklessness, as invincible as I was. This wasn't a car, this
was a *tank*! And now it was a tank sinking in not one foot
but *four* feet of water.

The road, it turned out, dipped significantly, but it was
impossible to see this with the rainwater covering the
ground. The car got maybe a third of the way through the
puddle before the water washed over the hood, and it stalled.
I immediately tried to restart, which only served to fill every
cylinder with runoff and short out the electronics.

This was a problem.

Like any good leader, I solicited advice from the other
team members, all of them educated, analytic adults attending one of America's top universities. Unfortunately, we
knew dick about cars. Joe suggested that we push the car. I
suggested that the water was probably over his head—Joe
was pretty short. Holly calmly, then not so calmly, observed
that water was seeping in under the doors. For a brief moment, hysteria reigned.

Very brief, though. Like I said, this was a good Road Trip
team, and any good Road Trip team functions well in an

emergency. We all knew our number-one priority: Save whatever items we could. It was still pouring and the water was still rising, but since we were under the overpass, it was dry and safe on the car's roof. My teammates quickly climbed up there and Holly called a tow truck on her cell. I passed up the vital electronics (camera, charger, laptop) and box after box of collected items.

By the time we got everything on the roof, the water inside was up to my chest. Fortunately, the tow truck showed up before I actually drowned. Unfortunately, the tow-truck driver was clearly not accustomed to helping people in emergencies come to terms with their loss. The first words out of his mouth were, "Wellll, that car'll never run agin." Truly, he knew how to comfort the grieving. The second thing he said was, "Since you're already wet, can you hook up the tow cable under the car?" A natural empath, no doubt.

Once the tow truck had dragged the car over to a side street, it drained pretty quickly. However, everything inside smelled like shit and swamp, and we desperately needed dry clothes. I called my insurance company and told them I had been in a totally unforeseeable "flash flood." Then we called home base and told them of the catastrophe. This hit the team on campus pretty hard—you can't win a Scav Hunt without a successful Road Trip, and we still had a day's worth of items to collect.

We managed to find a Christian consignment store, which we entered wearing mostly just our (wet) underwear. The old ladies running the place were nearly apoplectic until Birge managed to explain our situation.

"We got trapped in that awful storm!" Birge told them, widening her eyes. "This is my first time in Illinois, and I had no idea it could rain so hard here. Thank goodness we found your shop—otherwise I just don't know what we would have done!"

Birge was cute, so the old Christian ladies believed her. They also, fortunately, didn't know just how much sacrilege we had committed over the past day. We bought some new clothes for a few bucks and returned to the stinky heap that was once my car to see what we could salvage.

The folks back at HQ assumed that this catastrophic setback meant the end of our Road Trip. One could only expect that with thousands of dollars of damage, with no functioning car, and with a huge time and distance gap to close, we would turn for home and cut our losses. This was the only rational response.

People who do Scav Hunt are many things, but rational is not one of them. Within an hour, we had secured a rental car (tough when you're all under twenty-five and broke), transferred our collected items into it, and, after a short eulogy for the departed, were back on the road.

I'm a Road Trip guy. I did it for all four years of college. And I hope that I never turn into the kind of person who does the smart and rational thing over the cool and crazy thing. I killed a car for the Hunt, and by God I'd do it again. What do you think about that, Jesus?

Doug Diamond graduated in 2004 with a degree in ancient studies (history of the ancient Near East). He Scavved for the Shoreland in 2001 and 2002 and for the FIST in 2003 and 2004. He is now a senior consultant for the Huron Consulting Group, working in healthcare IT, with a focus on data analytics in the healthcare space.

DOUG DIAMOND'S STORY ABOUT PEEING ON THE TEN Commandments is neither the first nor the last time that Scavvies thumbed their noses at organized (or even disorganized) religion. Here are some others.

19 ITEMS THAT WERE ONLY SLIGHTLY BLASPHEMOUS, HONEST

1987.104: A communion wafer (NO teeth marks allowed). [20 points]

> The genesis of one of the Hunt's earliest fiascos. Most teams did the rational thing and went to an ecclesiastical supply store downtown where you could buy unconsecrated wafers in huge cracker packs. One team, however . . . didn't.
>
> Following the Hunt, an annoyed member of the clergy contacted Hunt organizers to ask why some darn college kids had swiped the body of Christ from their church that weekend. It was left to Chris Straus, Hunt founder, to seek appropriate penance in the form of receiving a private sermon on the topic.

1990.283: Church bulletins, dated May 13, 1990, from five different Hyde Park churches. (You'll probably need to go for confession anyway.) [15 points]

1993.190: A rabbi. [25 points + 30 bonus points if he can dunk OR + 5 bonus points if he tries]

> You'll note that a basketball is not mentioned in this item. The Judges graciously allowed the rabbis present to earn the extra points by dunking a (certified Kosher) doughnut in milk.

1994.168: "Nun Run": bring a nun in full habit to participate in a short foot race. This race will be conducted at 1:00 PM on the day of the judging. [100 points for first place, descending to minimum of 25 points]

> Teams found that getting the full habit was much more difficult than finding willing nuns, many of whom were U of C alumnae.

1994.68: A man, a woman, a live snake, a red apple, leaves, NOTHING ELSE [69 points]

> Judges at the time remarked that they wished they had emphasized the "leaves" aspect a bit more strongly.

1995.97: A Mormon named Norman [11 points]

> Notably, one team completed this item, in a feat of true Scavvie ingenuity, by going to a Mormon temple, waiting for the service to let out, then yelling "HEY, NORMAN!" until someone turned around.

1996.23: A rabbi eating sushi. [32 points.]

1999.59: A signed picture of Jerry Falwell or any other religious Zealot. [5 points]

2003.206: Break all Ten Commandments in one, damning action. [10 points]

2004.144: Corinthians 13:1—*If I speak in the tongues of men and of angels, but have not love, I am only a resounding gong or a clanging cymbal.* Cupid, in Greece, is called Eros, but since this is The Passion of The Scav Hunt, we'll call him Little Agape, and, demonstrating our more progressive religious developments, we won't require single gender characterizations. Beginning Thursday morn all will rejoice as Little Agape descends onto our earthly campus to induce periphesence at will, or at the holy command of the Judges. He is omnipresent, omniscient. Remember that even in the most conservative depictions, our angel only wears a cloud or two. Little Agape should also be equipped with a bow, arrow dipped in his or her heart-shaped flask of ambrosiac Agape Potion #9, and prepped Hallmark-esque cards for composition and delivery. Teams are thereby encouraged to love thy neighbor, or fall victim to the pang of Agape's archery. [131 points]

> Scavvies wandering around campus wearing clouds and carrying bows and arrows were a common sight the entire weekend.

2005.85: Though the battle of Terri Schiavo was lost, the War against people against people of Faith will certainly be won. But we must never forget the fight for the freedom to have political operatives free us from the freedom to free ourselves from our earthly vessels, as according to John 11:4. Thus you must cast a memorial bronze of our Terri in her last days of sufficient size to hold down the paperwork for our most recent Indian Casino lobbying venture. [38 points]

> Terri Schiavo, you may recall, was a woman in an irreversible vegetative state who had been at the center of a right-to-die legal battle that came to a head shortly before the 2005 Hunt.

2006.255: "Hint of Lime" communion wafers [1 point]

> Clearly, by this point, the lessons of 1987 had been forgotten.

2006.270: Who said they are ALL blasphemous? A non-sacrilegious image of يبن from a 15th century مرجانمة. Must be riding بوراق. [4 points]

> A reference to some of the few nonsacrilegious images of Mohammed that can be found in fifteenth-century illuminated texts, where he can be seen riding his flying horse, Buraq.

2007.8: The official exorcist of the Archdiocese of Chicago. If you're seeking legitimacy, remember that possession is nine-tenths of the law. [The Holy Trinity of points]

2008.154: Your take on a Bedouin Wedding feast. Points per strictly nested at least one inch long vertebrate of a unique species. Bonus points for species not native to North America. Bonus points for any hugably cute animal. Bonus points if deep fried. Bonus points if roasted on a spit. Bonus points if wrapped in bacon (because everything is better wrapped in bacon). Bonus points if John Madden describes how to open it. Bonus points for real Bedouins. Bonus points for real wedding. Bonus points for each major world religion banned from partaking. Bonus points if you can demonstrate any animal is genetically modified. Bonus points if final animal is biting an apple. No points if inedible. Bonus points if we think it's tast-e. [75 points, plus up to 50 bonus points]

> Scav Hunt Judges have rarely if ever identified a culture that they are unwilling to appropriate, if they think it will make for a good item.

2009.17: Out of love for the truth and the desire to bring it to light, pick a department and put it on notice that you have a few matters you'd like to dispute. Take a picture of your handiwork before you're excommunicated. [15.17 – 9.5 points]

> A reference to the wording and posting of Martin Luther's *Ninety-Five Theses* on a church door. If there's one thing U of C students have on hand, it's a spare thesis or two.

2010.10: Job globe. When shaken, biblical tragedies occur. Why, God, why?! [9 points]

2012.66: Maybe the Church of Satan is having trouble catching on because they don't have any of those fun worksheets for kids to color and solve puzzles in during Black Mass. Help them out by designing one, and please use proper sources for your information. Our children are our future! [2.666 points]

2015.256: On THURSDAY at 5:00 p.m., come to HUTCH COURTYARD for BIBLEMANIA UofC I! Make sure your pro wrestlers act out a specific interpersonal conflict from either the Old or New Testament when they step into the ring. Five minutes per match and one match per team. Your victor must walk out with a championship belt. [20 points]

> Notable acts included Jesus vs. The Fig Tree, Jesus vs. Paul the Lesser, and Moses vs. Pharaoh vs. Slave Runner Triple Threat Match.

LEST YOU THINK SCAVVIES ARE SIMPLY A BUNCH OF heathens, please note that it's not only religious traditions that they are willing to mess with. As the following essay shows, they will literally deface their own bodies if there are points to be had.

ITEM 58:

THE GIRL WITH THE INFAMOUS TATTOO

Cristina Romagnoli

2004 SCAV HUNT

In the years immediately following college, when people would see the heart-shaped tattoo of questionable taste scratched shoddily into my right hip, they assumed that behind the needle there must be a debauched tale that ended a tequila-filled night in a seedy parlor with an "artist" with a name like Bubba. These days, gravity, stretch marks, and the rather subpar application of my "work of art" have rendered the words that make up the heart almost entirely illegible, which is fine by me.

If they are sharp-eyed enough to notice that the heart is made up of text, however, people ask, "What does it say?" with a polite but slightly perplexed look on their face. I briefly consider quoting some overplayed Backstreet Boys anthem, just to seem culturally acceptable, but in the end I always tell the truth about the sentence that makes up my tattoo.

Sometimes, after I say it, the conversation ends abruptly with a head tilt, some rapid blinking, a very confused face, and an excuse to leave as soon as possible.

Others laugh awkwardly, change the subject, and never speak of it again.

Future friends, unfazed, will enquire: "Yeah, but what does it say in the middle?"

Gratified by their curiosity and nihilistic attitude toward an objectively distasteful tattoo, I happily reply:

"'SCAV 2004'!"

I stepped up to get this tattoo for Shoreland's 2004 team. Even more ridiculous, I didn't step up alone; in fact, I was handcuffed to my teammate Nicolle for the four days, which is a whole other adventure story. So, in the middle of the afternoon, just over the state line into Indiana, four legs, a set of silver bracelets, and forty bucks got the world's most ridiculous tattoo. The artist initially laughed when I told him what I wanted it to say. He was also a bit concerned about the idea of tattooing someone handcuffed to another person. When he realized I was serious, he furrowed his brow and then ultimately suggested red for the piece. "Red," he said flatly, "will be much easier to cover up after the fact." The idea was to make it heart-shaped so I could fill it in after the hunt, and no one would ever have to know what it had said. After signing some papers, and triple-checking that I was serious, he etched the red heart tattoo on my right thigh. For which our team was awarded the full 69 points, I might add!

Many people know this story now, but no one ever asks me *why*. Why did I get this absurd and permanent inscription on my own body? Was I wrapped up in the excitement and frenzy of the weekend? *Yes, but that is not why.* Was tequila actually involved? *Yes—well, some—but that is not why.*

For years I was uncomfortable trying to explain it, but now at last I feel like I can.

Although my team may have been using me for those coveted 69 points, I in turn was using Scav Hunt to regain a sense of personal power. I had transferred to the U of C as a second year with some marks on my body, marks that had been placed there without my consent. About two years earlier, three men had attacked me as I walked home from my closing shift as a bartender at a vodka bar called Revolution in Manchester, England. It was only six months after that I decided to transfer from the University of Manchester to the University of Chicago. I couldn't be there anymore. Externally, many of the visible scars had healed, but still my physicality, my body, was not my own.

One night not long before Scav Hunt began, I was walking on campus, nervously toying with a scar on the soft part of my left forearm, when I saw our beautiful phoenix crest and simply began to cry. I wondered to myself—*could it be that I, too, am here to rise again?*

The night our team was reading through the newly acquired List, I was fussing with that same scar, as I often did, when my ears perked up at the word "tattoo." Later that night, when Nicolle, cuffed sweetly to my right side, was sleeping, I looked at that mark on my body. It was then that I decided I would make a mark of my own.

To this day, that hideous red splotch on my right thigh is my one and only tattoo. I never considered getting one before the item came up, and I have never since wanted another. And despite the tattoo artist's saying that red is easy to cover up, and that the heart outline would be easy to fill in, I never did modify it. The tattoo remains just as it was on that Judgment Day. It is the first mark I chose for myself after many had been chosen for me, and to this day it reminds me of my power to choose.

Oh, yeah, and if you are wondering what it says . . . well, here's the item:

58. A permanent tattoo (we're talking the real deal) that reads, "Sorry about the syphilis, can we still be cousins?" [69 points]

Cristina Romagnoli graduated in 2006 with a dual concentration in visual arts and archaeology. She participated in Scav from 2004 to 2006. Cristina is a doctor of physical therapy who specializes in the treatment of the oncology and lymphedema populations. She is passionate about total mind and body wellness and integrates mindfulness and her training as a yoga teacher into the care of all her patients.

CRISTINA ROMAGNOLI'S STORY ABOUT USING SCAV TO reclaim her body is sobering and powerful. At the same time it is also inherently ridiculous, because of what the tattoo says and, of course, because of Nicolle. Nicolle was there the whole time—they couldn't go anywhere else. But even as they and their teammate were never more than a couple feet apart, Nicolle was going through their own process and having an entirely different experience. Here's *their* story of those same four days.

ITEM 133:

DOES THEIR RELATIONSHIP LACK TRUST?

Nicolle Neulist

2004 SCAV HUNT

133. Does their relationship lack trust? Bring two non-Apprentice, non-Captain, non-All Star teammembers to the center of the Quads at 10:00 AM on Thursday and let us test this friendship. [the strength of this friendship will determine the points]

How do you test the strength of a friendship you don't have?

Cristina and I had just met earlier that day, but we were the only two people on the Shoreland team who were willing to show up for this item. The best strategy either of us could come up with, at a few minutes before 10:00 a.m. on Thursday, was to share the answers to biographical questions. How old are you? Where have you lived? How many siblings do you have? Do you have a significant other? What is your concentration?

Head Judge Kaury arrived with a bag in her hand. Relief coursed through me when she pulled out a pair of handcuffs and proclaimed that each pair would have to be chained together for the duration of the Hunt in order to get full points on the item. That we could do. Though we knew almost nothing about each other, we knew the one thing that mattered for this item: that we were both enthusiastic enough about Scav Hunt to test our friendship with a complete stranger.

We didn't hesitate. I was left-handed, Cristina right-handed. I stuck out my right wrist, she stuck out her left, and the Judges clasped on the cuffs. They melted wax into the keyhole, as a seal, in case either of us had a spare key or was a little handy with a paper clip. That was that. We would be Scavving together for the next four days.

* * *

We began figuring out the logistics of our daily life together. Going to class was the easiest part: we didn't. I had been planning to work a few hours during Scav, but gluing pockets into library books is hardly a time-sensitive endeavor. A quick email to my boss pushed those hours into the following week, and I didn't even have to confess that sticking to my original schedule would have required grabbing a chair for a captive new coworker.

Everything else was a little awkward, but we kludged it together. Since I was living on my best friend's couch off campus, we slept in Cristina's room in Shoreland. I've always been a side sleeper who tosses and turns, but the handcuffs forced me into sleeping on my back, as still as I could, for a few hours a night. Fortunately, Scav doesn't involve much sleeping anyway. We took turns showering. I stood in the shower, shirt and bra hanging from the chain between our wrists, curtain pulled up to my dangling right arm, washing myself with my free hand as Cristina stood just outside. Then we switched. Going to the bathroom was similar. We both got in the stall, and whoever needed to go went while the other stood in the few spare square feet left in the stall, looking away.

Even though we spent Thursday on a wild dash around the city doing items, the real madness happened when we paused for meals. We visited a record store in Lincoln Park, trying (in vain) to find a record with more than one groove on a side for item 195, then stopped across the street for a hot dog at the Wiener's Circle. I expected a calm, quick bite to eat, but when we reached the counter, the cashier looked at our handcuffs and screamed: "Are you trying to make some bold lesbian political statement?!"

"Oh, no, this is for a scavenger hunt!" I explained in as bubbly a voice as I could muster. I had come out of the closet as bisexual less than a year before, so being so brashly faced with That Queer Stuff while handcuffed to a stranger frazzled my nerves. Still, I called it a success. Eventually the Wiener's Circle folks stopped yelling at us, Cristina didn't destroy the handcuffs and run the other way, and we sat down and ate our hot dogs—me with my left hand, her with her right.

★ ★ ★

We went northwest, told the Metra what we thought of it (item 168), then made our way back to Hyde Park. Before returning to headquarters at Shoreland, we needed dinner. We ducked into Maravillas for a little Mexican food. About halfway through our meal, a Chicago police officer lumbered up to our booth and said, in a gruff yet nasal tone, "We had reports that there were people at Maravillas handcuffed together and naked."

We explained that the handcuffs were for a scavenger hunt, we had consented to the shackles, and we had been fully clothed for our whole meal. Had he been a University of Chicago police officer, this would have been easier; after all, the UCPD was well accustomed to broadening their definition of "civic order" for four days in May. City cops were less familiar with our mayhem.

Eventually satisfied that no indecent exposure had happened, the confused officer left us to finish our meal in peace. We cleaned our plates and turned to leave for headquarters. At the booth nearest the exit, two men sat across from each other. The man with his back to the door had an open Bible in front of him and looked across the table with a paternal-istic air. His student looked back at him quietly. Obediently.

As we walked past the table toward the exit, the older man turned glazed eyes up toward us. His voice was flat. "Why are you handcuffed together?"

After the conversations with the Wiener's Circle cashier and the policeman, we had our elevator pitch down. "It's for a scavenger hunt!"

"God has his own scavenger hunt," the man told us. "He's hunting for lost souls."

He tilted his head back down toward the Bible. He turned the page.

* * *

We were not naked at Maravillas on Thursday. The officer did not need to know that I'd be showing a bit more skin the next day, at the Seminary Co-Op bookstore. You were not allowed to carry any bag of any size into the co-op; the cashier at the front desk insisted on checking every bag from every person who walked into the store. So the Judges created item 14, which was to go in there wearing nothing *but* bags.

Without the handcuffs in the way, this would have been easy enough: shove my clothes in a book bag, cover a few parts of my body with other bags, and head into the store. While handcuffed? I could remove my pants, socks, and shoes, but my pesky shirt and bra swung from the chain connecting me and Cristina.

None of the clerks said a thing as we walked in there. We gallivanted around the shop with a teammate who took pictures, including the one that will forever define Scav for me. My right hand remains shackled to Cristina, a maroon T-shirt (saying "The University of Chicago: Where the squirrels are cuter than the girls!") and a white bra hanging from the chain of the handcuffs. Book bags separate me from indecent exposure, barely. My left hand holds up a pink book: Michael Warner's *The Trouble with Normal*. A grin lights my face.

✦ ✦ ✦

I have sixteen Scav Hunts behind me now. In all that time, the only item I regret not doing was also on the List that year—a tattoo that said, "Sorry about the syphilis, can we still be cousins?" I didn't have any tattoos yet, and at the time the thought of getting one felt too permanent. Still, I ended up peripherally involved in that tattoo item, thanks to the handcuff item. Because one person on Shoreland's team had the moxie to get the ink: Cristina.

We piled into the car: Cristina and I, along with our teammate, Alex. Alex was driving because he wasn't handcuffed to anyone. He also had a few tattoos already, so he would be able to tell whether a tattoo shop was sanitary or if we needed to bail out and find another one. We hit the road to Whiting, Indiana. There are plenty of good tattoo parlors in Chicago, but this was during Illinois's brief, failed experiment of raising the tattoo age to twenty-one. Cristina was twenty, so we had to go to an over-eighteen state.

The small shop, clean and neat, passed muster. We explained the tattoo and the scavenger hunt to the artist. He was entertained, but not as bemused as one would expect. I guess that, over the course of his career, this was not the strangest request he had ever accommodated.

Cristina sat in the chair, hip exposed. The needle buzzed, driving red ink into her skin, forming the words in the shape of a heart's outline. The idea was that if she wanted to fill the tattoo in later, she could have a perfect red heart instead.

As the artist worked on Cristina, my phone buzzed in my back pocket. I used my free hand to see who it was. A 208 area code. Boise, Idaho. My mother.

I had two choices: I could pick up the phone and try

to explain that I couldn't talk much now because I was in Whiting, Indiana, handcuffed to a woman I hardly knew, while she was getting a tattoo about syphilis. Or I could let the call go to voicemail and just ring her back the next day. Mother's Day.

I chose option B.

* * *

How do you test the strength of a friendship you don't have?

By the time the Judges extricated the wax from the keyholes, let me and Cristina out of the handcuffs, and gave Shoreland full points for item 133, I had an answer. It didn't matter what our pasts shared or what they didn't share. It didn't matter that in the future, we'd be friendly but not close—Facebook friends, as we are to this day. It only mattered that we loved Scav Hunt enough to take up the challenge of spending four days at each other's sides. That one thing we had in common gave us all the strength we needed.

Nicolle Neulist (AB '04) has the words "political science" printed on their diploma, but it would be more accurate to say they double-concentrated in mock trial and Scav Hunt. Nicolle has Scavved for Woodward Court (2001), Max Palevsky (2002), Shoreland (2003–2005), and GASH (2008–present). When it's not the Four Days, Nicolle is a freelance horse racing writer and also works for Equibase as a chart caller at Hawthorne Race Course and Arlington International Racecourse. You can read more of their work at blinkers-off.com.

YOU MAY HAVE GATHERED THIS FROM THE COLLECTION of coleslaw items, but just to be clear: once Scav starts on a joke, they don't let it go. They will adapt it, modernize it, reverse the order of the words in it, create a pun item out of it, make a worse pun out of the first pun, and on and on. If you didn't think it was funny on the 2005 List, you definitely will by the 2025 List. And if you didn't "get it" the first time, that's fine, because eventually it will become so self-referential that there is nothing real to get. One of the best examples of this is the following series of Mike Royko items.

Mike Royko was a famed Chicago newspaper columnist and sixteen-inch softball fanatic, whom Studs Terkel once described as "possessed by a demon." Over his thirty-year career, Royko wrote over 7,500 columns for the *Chicago Daily News*, the *Chicago Sun-Times*, and the *Chicago Tribune*. In several of those articles, he referred to students at the University of Chicago as being stuffy, humorless, and self-important. Here is what Scav had to say about that.

16 ITEMS DOCUMENTING AN INCREASINGLY ESOTERIC FEUD WITH PULITZER PRIZE-WINNING JOURNALIST MIKE ROYKO

1987.209: Mike Royko's signature on the *Chicago Tribune*'s front page. [50 points]

> Apparently, enough Scavvies descended on Royko's office and his known hangout, the Billy Goat Tavern, that *Chicago Tribune* security staff was called. From that point forward, Royko would make it clear that he planned to be out of town whenever Scav Hunt time rolled around, often leading to the participation of his secretary being deemed a fair replacement.

1988.50: A picture of Mike Royko taken this weekend (i.e. date must be incorporated into the photo—e.g. the front page of a newspaper!). [250 points]

> This item was successfully completed with the help of Mike Royko of Marion, Indiana. Hence the future references to "of the *Chicago Tribune*."

1989.23: A pair of socks autographed by Mike Royko of the *Chicago Tribune* (go get 'em, guys!). [50 points]

A reference to Royko's move from the *Sun-Times* to the *Tribune*, where he claimed that the only thing he changed was his socks. This was a pivotal point in the Scavvie-Judge arms race, as one participant would start the legal process to change his name to "Mikeroyko Ofthechicagotribune." Scav Hunt rules would get increasingly specific as to the technical requirements of what item completions would receive points, eventually morphing to the current status of "You know what we wanted and we'll decide if we'll give you points for this instead."

1990.159: A letter by Mike Royko of the *Chicago Tribune*, on *Tribune* stationery, with a statement that "the University of Chicago is a Great Institute of Higher Learning and a Most Excellent Party Zone." [50 points]

1990.258: What was Mike Royko arrested for? [8 points]

Answer: His participation in a 1977 barroom brawl.

1991.156: A Mike Royko article that is complimentary toward the UofC, with his business card stapled to it. [40 points]

1992.210: A genuine piece of Mike Royko's stationery with the name and signature of his secretary. [70 points]

1993.157: A copy of Mike Royko's vacation itinerary for this year. Must be on *Tribune* letterhead. [15 points]

1994.83: A Mike Royko article translated into Pig Latin with his secretary's signature on it. [54 points]

1994.245: A packet of Royco chicken flavoring [15 points]

As in cheep-cheep-cheep-cheep-cheep-cheep!

1995.25: A realistic Mike Royko (*Chicago Tribune*) sculpture made of solder [17 points]

1996.60: An envelope, with postage paid, to be mailed to Mike Royko, with the message "Dear Royko, Having a great time, wish you were here! Luv, Scavenger Hunt." printed on a copy of an arrest report for a DUI/DWI enclosed. Return addresses to Genghis Kraken care of the RSO Office in Reynolds Club. [45 points]

> A somewhat below-the-belt reference to Royko's 1995 conviction for driving under the influence.

1997.272: A séance to contact the spirit of Mike Royko—adieu, sweet Royko, adieu . . . [65 points]

> Mike Royko died of a brain aneurysm on April 29, 1997. You would think we would have stopped there. But then . . .

1998.111: Royko Aneurysm Antipasto (Think it's tasteless? just add some salt). [5 points]

> After this probably unnecessary parting shot came a long period of lists without Royko items. However, as a new generation of Scavvies and Judges took form, the Scav community began to look back on the historic feud with fondness, making for a resurgence in Royko references:

2006.295: An actual, live, present, nonimpersonated famous person. University-affiliated persons not permitted.

> Level 1—Local celebrity (Chicago weather man, that Empire Carpet guy, Stephen Baldwin) [1 to 20 points]
>
> Level 2—Minor celebrity (former member of Mega-

deth, dude from MST3K, Daniel Baldwin) [21 to 50 points]

Level 3—National star (Senator Obama, Michael Crichton, Billy Baldwin) [51 to 100 points]

Level 4—International star (Kofi Annan, Arnold Schwarzenegger, Alec Baldwin) [101 to 200 points]

Level 5—Mike Royko, of the *Chicago Tribune*. [A bajillion points]

2009.194: The Apotheosis of Terkel. You know who should take the place of Nike (Hint: it's Mike Royko of the *Chicago Tribune!*) [27 points]

THE THING ABOUT SCAV IS THAT IT BOTH IS AND IS NOT
real life. It feels consequence-free, but of course, everything does
have its consequences. As Dave Muraskin points out, poison oak
rashes don't go away just because Scav Hunt is over. And as Jake
Eberts's story about the T-shirt cannon and Jennifer Joos's story
about the braille *Playboy* remind us, you still have to live with what
you've done, even if you did it for points.

Similarly, a real-life problem may be put on hold during Scav
Hunt, but it doesn't go away. In fact, sometimes, Scav only makes
it worse. That's what happens in this next piece. Please note that
this essay includes discussions of emotional abuse, eating disor-
ders, suicidal thoughts, and self-harm. If you or someone you know
is struggling, please reach out to trained professionals like the National Eating Disorder Association (800-931-2237) or the National
Suicide Prevention Lifeline (800-273-8255).

ITEM 229:

THE FINAL FEAST

Naseem Jamnia

2013 SCAV HUNT

"Are you doing Scav?" he asks me. My answer at that time is no. It is a lie, although I do not know it then.

His name is Nick, and I fall in love with him over the course of my first year. Like me, he's a premed, both of us hoping to do an MD/PhD after graduation. Like me, his life is defined by a drive to understand a disorder: for him, hemophilia; for me, autism. We live in South Campus, both on dorm council and in the same math class. He claims to have burned his taste buds off with hot sauce, and I learn to increase my spice levels.

For years, we are inseparable. For years, people ask how the other is doing whenever they see one of us. For years, our favorite memories, the ones that really keep us together, are from Scav.

Without Nick, I never would have been a Scavvie or a captain. I never would have befriended Judges, met people from across the dorms, learned the limits of my endurance. Scav taught me teamwork, dedication, sacrifice, and friendship.

At least, I think it did.

229. For Scavenfeast 2014, the surprise is inside. Every culture has their version of dumpling, from Italian ravioli to Indian samosas to corn dogs, but traditional combinations are so played out, so take the outside of one type of dumpling and pair it with the filling for another. Equally, every culture has a canonical pair of items that are really one dish at heart, so make it so! Take a dish like fish and chips, wine and cheese, or soup and salad and combine it into one cohesive unit. To finish, remember that the surprise is inside when you present us with an edible piñata. Please join us with your culinary creations in McCormick Tribune Lounge at 6:30 p.m. on Saturday. [ω points]

It's 2013, my last Scav (which the Judges have inexplicably decided to refer to as "the 2014 Scav Hunt," mostly so that they can refer to the next year as "the second annual 2014 Scav Hunt"). I am one of my team's captains for the second year in a row. I come into this, my fourth year, my last year, with hope.

Sort of.

I am glad to be a captain again, though I'd idly contemplated applying for Judgeship. But we were so sure this would be Nick's year, and—with the support of the rest of the captains—he applied but was not brought into the ranks. He is a bitter captain this year. I will not remember most of it. Our team name will completely elude me when I try to recall it just a few years later. When I look at the List, I will pick out just four items that I was a part of. Where was I, this Scav?

This question whispers in my ear, repeats its refrain, because it's not just this Scav I do not remember, but the ones before it, either.

But I try to.

We are second years when Nick is first made a captain, in 2011, and the others tell me that I'm not also made one because Nick and I are the same. Still, I spend the months before Scav running fund-raisers and baking for him, as if by doing the work of a captain I can prove, too late, that I deserve the title. No matter how much of my money and time I pour into cupcakes and flyers, I do not win Nick's love.

So much of the lead-up to the 2011 Hunt fades from my mind. I know there are late nights in his room, scribbling in o-chem notebooks for the next day's lab. I know that he complains about his roommate, who seems unbothered by my constant presence. I know that around Halloween, he tells me he does not think he can feel love. I think, but do not tell him, that I can love him enough for the both of us.

There are fights here that I do not remember. I have to flip through old notebooks and emails to find remnants of what might have happened. *You need to be better than this*, he said to me once, as I stared at plates of food I was refusing to consume. Throwing a phone at me, before a national crisis hotline closed: *You have five hours to call*. A threat, a promise of his imminent anger when I once again fail to do as he bids.

When Scav Hunt 2011 rolls around, Nick dons the white shirt of the Greek god Osiris (item 62: "By Thursday morning, your team Captains reveal themselves as the living incarnations of the Egyptian pantheon"). I bite back of my jealousy and anger at his affection toward the other captains and teammates. His affection toward everyone but me. It fills me, the thrumming taste of his denial, of my obsession. He is a god, here, and we both know how far that extends.

Second year is the first where I take over Scavenfeast, make it the center of my Scav experience. At this time in my life, food is the center of all of my experiences. For a year, my stomach has shrunk, and my hair has been collecting at the bottom of the drains. I am in a clinical program now, attending twice a week to talk about my feelings around food. It is all I think about: how much I've eaten, what I've eaten, when I've eaten. I count the crumbs. Nick watches me deteriorate, but his method of saving me—asking what I eat, telling me to eat more, watching me take every bite—does the opposite.

When I go searching for these details years later, I find a transcript of a conversation we once had, the middle of the story I am constantly writing about us. The words do not surprise me, even though I can't remember them.

"You're fucking eating."

"Nick, I don't feel like—"

"I'm not leaving until you eat."

I take a bite of fruit. "Look, I'm eating!"

"That's not even a whole piece of melon! You have another thirteen pieces to go, and then you're eating a slice of pizza."

"No."

"Eat it. I'm not leaving until you do. I'm not going to eat until you do. You not eating makes me feel even more guilty than I already do."

And it is this threat that finally makes me acquiesce.

These fights will haunt me, follow me into classes and into Scav. And so I focus on Scavenfeast, close my hands around this item and make it my own.

Only the best for Scav: I take the item description to my dorm's Resident Master for advice. She prints out a brisket recipe that I will keep but never make again, the memories—and lack thereof—of the first attempt sapping my appetite. I spend $150 of Scav money to put together a feast that will impress the Judges. Nick chastises me for the receipt, as he is in charge of all money, especially mine.

On Saturday night, the linoleum floor of eX Libris Café bathed in an eerie light, we make brisket sandwiches to serve to the Judges. I man our table the full time and do not try anything we've made, although I hear it is delicious. I do not try the other teams' creations, either. But I sit and stare at the food, hunger burning in my belly, and wait.

Here is another memory, one of the few that burn brightly in my mind: A girl named Rachel creates *eau de Harold's chicken* (item 103: "Adorn yourself with your favorite scent, and bring me a sample for my own collection"). I do not smell it for fear that I will be sick. I remember that her name was Rachel because I remember the party that happens a week or two after Scav, when I walk in to see her sitting on Nick's lap, the two of them laughing. My stomach roils, and the host mixes me something called a grasshopper. I take a few sips before I walk into the bathroom, lift the seat, and vomit.

When I ask Nick about it later, he just shrugs. We have already had The Talk a dozen times—What are we? Why don't you know? How do you feel about me? How am I supposed to get over you when you treat me differently from everyone else? How are we just friends when I love you, and you let me? Nothing changes: his emotional distance but insistence at my openness; the demand of my thoughts when he gives none of his own; the fury that I would dare hide something from him—whether it's skipping a meal, having depressive thoughts, or, once, the flashes of what my death might look like—when he never shares his true feelings. I want to know why a Scavvie is allowed to sit on his lap when I am not allowed to hug him. He can't make it make sense to me. And he doesn't try.

Our second year ends. Third year is the longest. Five months before Scav 2012, I wrap a telephone cord around my neck and contemplate. Four weeks before Scav 2012, I set out pills and write Nick a text goodbye. He is in class. I go to shower, wondering if I can stop myself from this permanent solution with a razor—and when the urge does not fade, I'm grateful that I'll at least be clean when I'm found. But he asks a friend to check in on me, and she walks in right before it's too late. That night, Nick bandages my legs as I say nothing. He is furious.

Sometime in the year—Facebook later confirms that it is in March, though I remember it in November—someone utters the phrase *emotional abuse* to me for the first time. I'm borderline offended, because how could I possibly have missed such an impossible thing, were it true?

I spend the year excited for Scavenfeast, the one thing I know I can do right. When I am handed three pounds of alligator meat, I decide to go to my roots for the dish, the Persian flavors I learned at my mother's elbow. I shop for eggplant, tomato paste, onions. I sprinkle turmeric and add saffron. It is my own taste of home—the Sufi center I was raised in, on the North Side of Chicago.

I am settled into recovery now, but Nick does not think so. He still demands to know about my eating, even though I've told him that my therapist, whom I see three times a week, says she wants me to stop discussing it with him.

Later, after the Hunt is over, Head Judge Leah will send the captains an email. She will say that the alligator I prepared was the best that she had that night. I will keep this in my inbox, to remind myself of the time that my cooking—and by extension, me—was, finally, enough.

Nick and I sublet an apartment together for the summer, where I work reception at the gym and he pretends to go to his research lab, but often skips out. He is kind to me, except when I am suicidal. Then he is stern and unforgiving.

That summer, we close the door to his room for privacy of a more nefarious kind, our relationship treading into physical waters for the first time, despite years of people suspecting otherwise. The first time it happens, he tells me that I'm not allowed to tell anyone, not even my therapist, and that it won't happen again. But it does. Several times.

Shortly before the school year begins, as I demand once again to know what we are, what I am to him, why he won't give me the love I want, he takes a sticky note and scribbles on it, not looking at me: *I can't because I'm attracted to guys. I'm sorry. I never wanted to be this way.* He takes it to the stove and burns it after I begin to cry.

My world is shattered. The next morning, I go to work drunk. I call my best friend from high school to meet up in a downtown Starbucks and I write out what his note said, wailing into her shoulder as she holds me. I think back on all the times someone asked if he was gay, then assumed he wasn't when they saw us together, all the times I threatened to "kill him" if he ever came out to me, like so many of the men I'd fallen for in the past. Suddenly, his denial of me throughout the years makes sense, and I am confronted with all of the ways he's lied: the girls he has claimed to have feelings for, instead of me; the half-hidden words whenever he said his feelings for me were complicated. Have I forced him into something he hasn't wanted, these last weeks of summer?

And those are the questions I must put aside as I face my final Scav, my final feast. And again the memories fade, but there is one thing about my final Scav that I do remember: Nick tells me I should not do Scavenfeast. Even though it is the one item that I know I can do each year, the one thing in which I take pride, for I am otherwise a useless Scavvie. He tells me I have been too controlling of it in previous years, that I need to let go. I don't argue that I've only ever done the main dishes. Instead, I hand the role to another captain, who creates a coffee-and-cigarette-inspired main dish. That's all I remember. I stand at the table where we present our food to the Judges, but I am not really there.

At this time, I'm dropping all of my responsibilities, forgetting everything that I need to do, just trying to make it to the end of the school year. I have applied to speak at graduation, and Nick is on the committee that will choose the three speakers. I am number four, *but everyone really liked your speech.* I am afraid that Nick will stop talking to me once we graduate, once he heads to Bethesda to work and I stay in Chicago to get a master's degree.

The psychiatrist I begin to see the fall of my fourth year says, within twenty minutes of meeting me, that Nick is the root of my problems. I don't believe him. *Depression runs through my family,* I insist. *He's my best friend,* I counter. *I am the one who's been in love with him, has forced him to care for me. He's always said no whenever I've told him my feelings.*

Nick tells me that this so-called doctor is an idiot. And for years, this so-called doctor will listen to the stories of our fights, where I make sure to blame myself, and tell me after every one that I need to set boundaries. He will be the cement in my mind that our relationship is unhealthy, that it is toxic, that I need to leave. He will be the one to tell me that *dreams are just dreams* when Nick begins to haunt them, that it doesn't matter if no one else believes *because it is our truth.* He will be the one who says, *You need to end this* after my final fight with Nick two years later. He does not use the word trauma, but others do.

And in all of this, I do see one truth: my Scav memories are twined deeply with a man who did not love me. And because Scav is so connected to him, and because I have blocked out so much about my relationship with Nick, I don't remember much about Scav, either. But there are little things that stay. The Etch A Sketch within an Etch A Sketch (2010, item 258), which I stay up all Saturday night to finish, shaking and reshaking until I can get as many iterations as possible on a tiny Etch A Sketch from Walgreens. A steel-wool Skarmory (2011, item 127), which Nick and I stay up all Saturday night working on with another captain, our fingers burning and cut from the process. Thirty-four hats stacked tall on my head (2012, item 194), on Judgment Day. A part of me was there for all of this, but I think I lost that part some time ago.

Naseem Jamnia attended the University of Chicago from 2009 to 2013, and they Scavved all four years for the team then known as South Campus. They also captained the team in 2012 and 2013 after baking a lot of fund-raising cupcakes. A member of first Wendt and then Jannotta House, Naseem majored in the biological sciences and minored in creative writing. After the 2016 election and a semester in a neuroscience PhD program, they left to pursue full-time freelance writing and editing, as well as work on their novels, and are beginning an MFA program in the fall. Naseem currently lives with their husband, dog, and two cats in Reno, NV, and can be found at www.naseemwrites.com.

NASSEM JAMNIA WRITES BRAVELY AND CANDIDLY about a difficult period in their life. One of the aspects of their piece that I find especially affecting is how they focus more and more on feeding others, for points, as their own refusal to eat overtakes their life. When I read Naseem's story, I see how Scavenfeast becomes a way for them to exercise control over food, to use food as a means to an end, to take pride in food without the anxiety of consuming it. Being "the person who handles Scavenfeast" becomes an integral part of their identity, which makes it all the more hurtful when that role is taken away.

Scavenfeast is a relatively recent addition to the Hunt's schedule, but there's a long history of the complex relationship between Scav and food. What follows is a lighter take on how that conflict can play out.

ITEM 123:

WE WERE SURVIVORS

Connor Coyne

2001 SCAV HUNT

Dig, if you will, the premise. It was 2001. Recent years of
Scav Hunt had witnessed a general consolidation of small
house teams into larger, monolithic dorm teams. My own
team—Mathews House—had been one of the last to fall,
finally giving in and joining up with their former archrivals
of Burton-Judson. Now living in a huge-but-gross off-campus
apartment on Hyde Park Boulevard, I felt cut off and preoc-
cupied with besting my thesis and Romanian test so I could
graduate on time (spoiler: I didn't). My girlfriend, Jessica,
was also ambivalent about returning to her old team in the
Shoreland.

We were joined in our discontent by the former cast and
crew of University Theater's winter production of Brecht's
The Caucasian Chalk Circle. This crowd was an unruly bunch
of misfits; all winter we had taken road trips and formed
bands together, and we still gossiped shamelessly on our
listhost. "Who's doing Scav Hunt?" we asked between gutter
jokes and UT rumormongering. "I'd like to, but I don't really
like my dorm team." "I like my dorm team but I only have
about five minutes for it this year." "I like my dorm team
and I have plenty of time, but I only want to play for a team

where we wear A-shirts as our official uniforms." "Hey, let's start our own team!"

Thus the Lush Puppies were born out of a lot of piss and vinegar and completely at the last minute. Jessica and I served as cocaptains and we got the reluctant permission of my roommates to use the gross apartment as our HQ.

When I arrived with the List at one in the morning, the living room was packed with a couple dozen newly minted Puppies. Halfway through our read-through, we found an item that involved team members filling three empty one-gallon milk jugs with pee. After multiple rereads of the List today I can't find that item, which absolutely baffles me—did we make up this item out of our own fevered imaginations? Was there some perfectly normal item that we somehow interpreted as a demand for pee jugs? Either way, we did it, and I can assure you that the results were far more toxic than the by-products of any working nuclear reactor. Curdled milk and stale urine are not happy roommates.

By dawn we were already delirious and spent, but still happy. Our strategy was simple: go crazy and do as much as we could. Town crier? Check. Classroom interruptions? Check. Road Trip? Why not. A techno performance of "The Devil Went Down to Georgia"? Yeah! And then there was this beaut:

123. Last year we intelligently, justifiably, and ceremonially cut the Who Wants to Be A Millionaire item. This year, unfortunately for some of you, we are not cutting the Survivor item. Each team, at 7h30 after the after the Captains' Meeting, must send a Survivor-savvy teammember to the island in the center of the quads for 34.5 hours of fun-filled excitement. Bring a luxury item that is not food, drink, or a chamber pot. Make it good. Furthermore, bring some day wear, some nightwear, a blindfold, and a tablet of paper with writing implements. Once you are on the island you have to stay on the island. And we know that you will snitch on your competitors. They, then, will snitch on you. Through immunity challenges, a sole survivor will remain. Finally, do not trash the flowers. [points, while huge, are TBA. 50 bonus points if you can have "Destiny's Child" sing for your winner]

A first year named Pat Kane volunteered for that item. Pat had been an ensemble member of *The Caucasian Chalk Circle.* He was a Chicago native, a South Sider from Beverly, with the stereotypical Irish and cop ancestry. My first impression of him had been that of a gentle giant, all the more so because he acted as the foil to his roommate Alex, a jester-like wit and raconteur. By Scav I had learned that there was more to Pat than the clichés, including his quiet but weird sense of humor and his basic stability in the midst of so many self-acknowledged drama queens (myself included). Still, edgy Alex seemed a better fit for the Dionysian free-for-all that the *Survivor* item promised.

But it was Pat who volunteered, and at 7:30 on Thursday morning I escorted him to the small grassy circle at the geographic center of campus, encompassed by an asphalt roundabout. I left him there with the Survivors from another ten teams and two Judges who were standing off to the side, grinning with an almost feral malignance.

After that, my own duties took over for a while. A captain wears many hats. We had to see our Road Trip off to Graceland. We had to prep our performance of "The Devil Went Down to Michigan." I personally had to interrupt my old Resident Head's lecture to scream "San Dimas High School Football Rules!" earning her everlasting enmity. Pat was on his own.

But Pat, it turned out, was in better shape than any of us. From the outset, he had two advantages.

First, the tangible: remember how I said that we were a small team in the midst of huge teams? We weren't a threat.

Nobody was in a hurry to kill off the Lush Puppies because nobody figured that the Lush Puppies were a serious rival in their quest for Scav glory.

Second, the intangible: among the betrayals of *Survivor*, Pat was a straight-up nice guy. He got along with everyone, didn't (seemingly) plot against anyone, played cards, told jokes, and commiserated under the tarp where the Survivors huddled during a chilly, rainy night. He relayed to us stories about how the Survivors had all held a rope, blindfolded, so that the Judges could begrudgingly lead them to a campus bathroom in the dark of the night to take care of nature's needs. And while Pat seemed to miss immunity challenge after immunity challenge, so he was continually up on the chopping block for his peers to evict, the vote always landed on someone else.

Back at HQ, we listened in delight and awe as we heard about Survivor after Survivor who had been exiled from the island. Now there were only six left . . . now only five . . . Twelve hours to go. Now there were four Survivors. Would Pat be next? Finally, only three. As the clock ticked, Pat waved down Jessica and relayed a message: "I think we can win this thing, if I can survive this round. If I get the immunity challenge, they'll bring back all of the Survivors to pick the winner. And I think they'll pick me."

Can you imagine? A Scavvie from a team so small, so new, triumphing over all those Goliaths, just by being a nice guy? This was my team! This was what the Lush Puppies were about!

The Judges announced the last immunity challenge. The three remaining Survivors were hungry from their day and a half on the quads. Each team was to prepare one meal that would be randomly assigned to one Survivor, and the Survivor who finished their meal first would win immunity.

It was up to me to make this meal. I rolled up my sleeves and got to work.

I'll admit that it occurred to me that there was a one-in-three chance that the meal I was preparing might be served to my own teammate. It even occurred to me that the decent thing to do would be to prepare something delicious and filling; whoever got it had been out in the elements and hungry. But while Scav Hunt isn't the Stanford prison experiment, and while I knew my team wasn't going to win, I felt no compunction to compete with the same sense of charity that Pat displayed on the quads.

My meal was a masterpiece. I made Bisquick pancakes according to the instructions, but using curdled milk and adding a generous helping of hot sauce to the mix. Then, as I stacked them on the plate, I heaped huge spoonfuls of salt onto the bottommost pancakes, hoping that that the sugar and Karo syrup I drizzled over the top would fool our rivals into taking huge bites. It was disgusting and foul, but as I carried the sticky feast to the quads, I kept trying to think about how it could be made even worse. When I met Alex on campus, I asked him what he thought.

"Oh, I have an idea," he said—of course he did, because he was Alex—and vanished with a teammate.

They returned a minute later with several grubs and wormlike larvae. We sprinkled them onto the pancakes. After some misgivings and the hairy eyeball from a Judge, we pulled off the grubs, but the worms had already burrowed into the spongy dough. It was too late to change course now: the Judges were calling for the meal.

You already know what happened next.

Of course each Survivor had to eat the meal prepared by their own team.

I don't know if the meal assignments were truly random

or not. I suspect not. When I lie awake at night, my brain echoing with the sounds of Pat's despair, I try to soothe my troubled conscience by reminding myself that the other two teams had also fed their comrades an eldritch concoction of vile, inedible rot. But I will forever be haunted by the expression on Pat's face in the moment before he took his first bite. A look of delight and appreciation for his teammates—for his captain—who had rewarded his loyalty and perseverance with some delicious pancakes on the eve of his *Survivor* victory.

Just as Icarus must have felt the sun's glow warm on his shoulders right before he plunged headlong into the sea, this reverie of camaraderie was doomed to a tragic end. Pat gagged on the first bite, but he swallowed. He shoveled in a second bite, and then a third. He kept going. I don't know if he was looking at me or not—I was looking at my feet in shame—but I imagined his warm, generous eyes burning into me with stunned anger at my betrayal.

I thought that this fiasco would end quickly. That one Survivor would vomit immediately, and that would trigger the same reaction in the others. But these were the hardened Three. They had lived by their wits on the quads for almost thirty-six hours, and so for many minutes the air was silent except for the scraping of forks and the groans of the afflicted. In the end, Pat finished, though nobody seems to remember who actually won the challenge. We all remember Pat throwing up, though. A horrible, miserable retching sound that drowned out the ambient sounds of traffic and trains.

Pat survived that final vote.

When his competitors returned to the island one last time, their vote was almost unanimous that Pat should carry the item. The Lush Puppies won. Jessica fired up a karaoke version of Destiny's Child to net us the 50 bonus points. Pat was nowhere to be seen, but the party on the quads was getting started now. A Scav captain wears many hats, and I was already pivoting toward the next challenge.

One of the Judges took me aside and said, "Whatever happens tomorrow, whatever happens Sunday, I just want you to know that you guys are in first place right now. Right now, you're ahead of everyone." In that moment, that was all I wanted to hear.

All Pat wanted, however, was a normal meal.

He didn't stick around for the party but decamped for 55th Street and delicious Thai food at The Snail. Remarkably, Pat got over his trauma and returned to Scav again the next year. Sometimes Scav Hunt demands a human sacrifice and Pat stepped up without flinching. By Friday night, Pat was more than just a nice guy. He was a survivor.

Connor Coyne, AB '01, G.S. Hum, Scavved for Mathews House from 1998 to 2000, cofounded the Lush Puppies in 2001, and went on to join Team Judge, from which he slowly climbed the ladder to the Elysian Fields of Scav. Today, he is a writer living in Flint, Michigan, with his Scav Hunt Judge wife, two Scavvie daughters, and a feisty adopted rabbit. You can find out more about his writing at connorcoyne.com.

EVERY JUDGE HAS A CERTAIN TYPE OF ITEM THAT they're known for writing, and mine is aggressively teeny-bopper items. The best-known example of this is the time I had Scavvies perform the choreographed dance from the Disney Channel's *High School Musical*'s "Stick to the Status Quo" in the dining hall (item 321, 2007). Watching this performance remains one of the high points of my Scav career and possibly my life; if you ever need true inspiration, I recommend getting two dozen college students to turn lunchtime into an immersive musical theater experience.

But I also strive to write items that could fulfill a Scavvie's dream just by asking for something they already have that they've never before realized was a useful asset. I think the closest I ever came to that was the "joint crack-off" (item 54, 2006), scored at half a point per audible joint crack, thirty-second time limit. In life, having joints that crack easily is at best unremarkable and at worst frowned upon. So what a delight to have that one day when your cracking joints are special, useful, called upon for the good of your team! How wonderful that this thing that you just *have* then becomes the thing that wins you points!

A grosser example of this sort of item is included in the following list—it's item 8, 2004. Is it even grosser than Pat eating a plate of grubs and spoiled milk? I'll leave that call up to you . . .

Fig. 1: One team's schedule of time-specific items and events. 2006. Photo credit Leila Sales.

Fig. 2: Cockfighting! Whichever frozen chicken still has his giblets duct-taped to him at the end of the marionette knife fight will be declared the winner. 2008. Photo credit Will Deitz.

Fig. 3: Ye Olde Socke 'Em Bopper Jouste. 2006. Photo credit
Leila Sales.

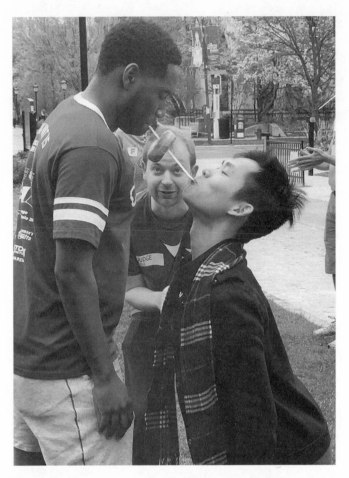

Fig. 4: Balance a doughnut on a slap bracelet "tongue" and successfully relay it to a teammate's slap bracelet tongue across the quads. If your bracelet snaps, you go back to the start. 2015. Photo credit Leila Sales.

Fig. 5: Last person left with a foam swim noodle still attached to their bike helmet wins. 2015. Photo credit Leila Sales.

Fig. 6: A wooden icon, adhering to the Orthodox Christian style, depicting reality TV star Honey Boo Boo. 2013. Photo credit Claire Gilbert.

Fig. 7: A simple, old-timey pie fight. 2008. Photo credit Will Deitz.

Fig. 8: Shopping cart archery, while dressed as characters from *The Legend of Zelda*. 2012. Photo credit Claire Gilbert.

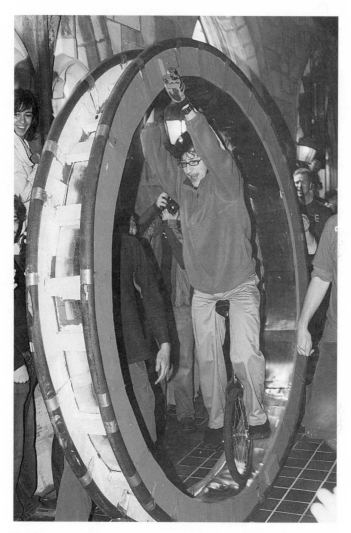

Fig. 9: A monowheel. 2008. Photo credit Will Deitz.

Fig. 10: Human lassoing. 2008. Photo credit Will Deitz.

18 ITEMS ABOUT FOOD

1987.74: The UofC's Chicken Kiev (aka fried hamster). [15 points]

> A reminder right from that start that, even at their most extreme, Scav Hunt eating challenges often paled in comparison to the cuisine usually offered at Pierce Dining Hall.

1988.127: A person who can eat a Harold's white half, with bread, fries and hot sauce—NO drinking during the event—must be done in under 4 min. Bonus points for under 3 1/2 min. and for 3 min. Teams must provide their own Harolds. [15, 20, 25 points, respectively]

> This is Harold's Chicken Shack, the bulletproof glass-ensconced South Side fried chicken chain so beloved by the U of C community.

1990.149: A team member who will stuff as many Dunkin' Donuts munchkins in his/her mouth as possible in 30 seconds. [3 points / munchkin]

> The record was seventeen.

1992.58: A team member covered in Rice Krispies. Pour one gallon of milk over the team member's head. Must snap, crackle, and pop. [56 points]

1993.1: Spotted Dick, to be eaten in front of the judge. [20 points]

1996.01: Target cheese log caber toss. Toss a cheese log caber-style (end over end) to an immobile teammate at least 20' away. If the teammate catches (Judge's interpretation) the cheese log, points will be awarded for distance. The cheese log must have a surviving section of at least 1" in length upon reception/impact. [10+ points for competing, 45 points for first place.]

1999.08: College Diet Staple Eat-Off. Needed: 43 flavor packs from ramen containers. Sure that's easy, but then there's the second part: crack open the containers, put them in a giant bowl, and pass that bowl around. Extra points if the last guy licks it clean. The entire relay must be done within five minutes. [50 points for first place, 25 for second, 15 for third]

2001.05: This is for y'all who wear fanny packs. You find your friend, a cheese-guzzling pig, and now the both of you have your chance to shine. Sure, we know that the highlight of cheese-guzzling was downing that bucket of nacho cheese at the cafeteria your sophomore year like it was a bucket of coleslaw. This, though, could beat it. The first teammember has to tie a fanny pack around his or her waist, with the pack up front. Now, into this pack, empty out 16 ounces of cottage cheese. Not that we're experts, but we suggest small curd. Race the other cheese-guzzling pigs on the other teams. You can only use the tools your mouth has—namely teeth, tongue, and fearsome sucking action. The person wearing the fanny pack can only use their hands as it pertains to running their fingers through the other person's hair. [50 points for first place, 25 for second, 15 for third. 15 bonus points if you finish the deed off with two tablespoons of Vegemite]

2004.8: A teammember's umbilical cord, to be eaten by that teammember. [96 points]

> The Scavvie who completed this item got his umbilical cord from his parents, stuffed it inside a Twinkie, and ate it.

2005.010: Harold and Kumarathon. Bring a case of White Castle Sliders and a PBR. First one done earns the title of "Non-Gendered Ruler of the White Castle" and a satisfied stomach.

> That is, incidentally, thirty sliders. There have been items in Scav's history that were technically more dangerous, but this stands out as the one that brought its participants closest to dying.

2006.09: What color is this food? What color *isn't* this food? I don't know, you tell me.

> Blindfolded participants were fed a number of different items, with difficulty ranging from "orange slices" to "purple cheddar-flavored Goldfish crackers."

2008.105: There's always room for Jell-O®! [50 points]

> In order to prove the contention of this item, at nearly every major Scav event that year, Scav Captains were given Jell-O to consume.

2009.256: Casu Marzu [11 points]

> A Sardinian delicacy, this is a ripe local cheese infested with maggots. These maggots can launch themselves with great force from the cheese, at distances of up to six inches, leading some to wear "maggot guards" when eating the cheese to prevent them flying up into your eyes.

2010.122: Place a cloth napkin over your head to hide your cruelty from the sight of God. Put the whole bird into your mouth, with only the beak protruding from your lips. Bite. Put the beak on your plate and begin chewing, gently. You will taste three things: First, the sweetness of the flesh and fat. This is God. Then, the bitterness of the guts will begin to overwhelm you. This is the suffering of Jesus. Finally, as your teeth break the small, delicate bones and they begin to lacerate your gums, you will taste the salt of your own blood, mingling with the richness of the fat and the bitterness of the organs. This is the Holy Spirit, the mystery of the Trinity: three united as one. It is cruel. And beautiful. Send your bravest gastronome to the entrance of Bond Chapel at 7:45 pm on Friday with napkin in hand. [Δ points]

> Though the wording suggests ortolan bunting (the possibly-mythical fowl dish that supposedly slices your mouth to deepen the flavor), those who arrived at Bond Chapel were treated to soft-boiled balut, an Indonesian street food that is made of partially incubated eggs.

2012.146: Play me a drink, Sam, for old times' sake . . . on your piano that dispenses a beverage component with every keystroke. Changing the melody should change the mixology. Instruments and their compositions will be judged both on the quality of the cocktails and the musicality of their recipes. [250 points, 25 extra points if your keyboard can play a different melody to create a different drink]

2015.247: Go clubbing. Get the DJ to play the Theme Song. Announce to all present that "THIS IS MY JAM!" At which point, distribute jars of delicious homemade preserves. [7 points]

> 2015's theme song was the aggressively not-jam "The Reason," by Hoobastank.

2016.232: A braided loaf of Cthallah, equal parts Kosher and Demonic Cult God. [6.86 points]

2017.01: THE MOST DELICIOUS GENTLEMAN'S DUEL: CHURRO FENCING. Tips of churro will be dipped in chocolate to mark the points on your special churro fencing outfit. Your special churro fencing outfit is a light-colored pillowcase with arm and head holes upon which you have Sharpied "Churro Fencing Outfit". Winner eats both churros and advances to the next round, competing yet again for glory and the gluttonous satisfaction of having eaten like 6 churros if they win the whole thing.

PARENTS UNDERSTAND THAT THEIR KIDS DON'T HAVE
time to call them during Scav Hunt. You hardly even have time
to go to the bathroom during Scav Hunt, and in some years I've
ended the weekend dehydrated because I was never willing to
leave headquarters for long enough to fill up my water bottle. But
as soon as Judgment is over, I do the good-daughter thing of calling
my mother to deliriously reassure her that I'm alive and wish her
a happy Mother's Day.

I have been involved with Scav on and off for fifteen years
now, and still my mom only partially understands it. However, because she is my mother, she is wildly supportive of it nonetheless.
Her favorite Scav story is about my team's completion of item 162
in 2005: http://www.theassbook.com.

That year's Hunt occurred just a few weeks after Facebook
had reached the U of C campus, but long before the site rolled
out to the public at large and became a social media behemoth.
My teammates' initial inclination, upon reading this item, was to
set up a social networking site with photos of butts. I disagreed; I
felt that it should be more like a hook-up directory, mapping out
who had made out with whom. (I maintain that this could be a useful, albeit horrifying, invention.) I have no computer coding skills,
but my teammate Yitz did, and he built the Assbook of my dreams.
Now the Assbook is no more—another casualty of the dot-com bubble burst, I suppose—and Yitz is a grown-up professional who does
something incredibly important and meaningful with computers.

My mother is extremely proud of theassbook.com, even
though I don't believe she has ever used the phrase "gotten ass,"
nor does she know how to log in to her own Facebook account.
Nonetheless, she brags about the Assbook as though it's one of
my major career achievements. Which, I don't know, maybe it is.

Some moms are just more understanding of Scav Hunt's pecu-
liarities than others. This next story is about a mom who took her
acceptance one step further . . .

ITEM 241:

GRACELAND, ALSO

William Wilcox
2013 SCAV HUNT

It was ten o'clock on Saturday morning as the cheap electric disco ball that could have been a prize at Chuck E. Cheese's turned on, slightly illuminating the room's boarded-up windows, walls covered in Elvis albums, and decrepit carpeting. I was coming to terms with the fact that I might be trapped inside the house of a mentally unstable Elvis aficionado who prided himself on his large stockpile of firearms, but before I get into that, I should probably explain how I got there.

It was for Road Trip. Of course.

I did the Road Trip for Snitchcock every one of my undergraduate years, so I can tell you from firsthand experience that the challenges of the Road Trip begin long before you leave campus. The first problem is finding a vehicle. Most U of C students don't own cars, and those who do don't usually want to loan them out for 2,000-mile round-trip drives to God knows where. Each year we go through two or three car volunteers who eventually back out because they can no longer convince their parents or extended relatives to lend them the car, or they realize what they're getting into.

Once you have the car, you have to find four drivers considered eligible by the university's standards. Clearing that hurdle has gotten harder over the years as other teams have crashed their cars, including Max P totaling a car because they saw "a really big raccoon." So beyond convincing four nerds to miss two days of class, which is hard enough, Snitchcock's fearless leaders have to get their drivers' spotless driving records proven and checked.

As the deadline for the 2013 Hunt approached, our captain Jay Cushing turned to the only person who would not possibly say no to him: his mother, Debbie. Debbie was indeterminately mom-aged and a hospital nurse in New England. She agreed to take time off from work to join us on our trip and drive the car herself to meet the insurance requirements. Felling multiple birds with one minivan, Debbie drove to Chicago all the way from her home in Maine.

Debbie knew that she would be driving cross-country with three young men she had never met before while her son stayed on campus to lead the team. She introduced herself to us over email with a photoshopped poster from the 1987 film *Three Men and a Baby* with our faces superimposed over the real actors and the text altered to read "Three Men and a Mommy." Though she noted in a follow-up email, "I will be shedding my mom-skin for this adventure. I can't wait to be a part of this team and have a blast. I don't want anyone to feel like I am supervising or judging or parenting in ANY way. I hope not to get arrested during RT, but I am otherwise up for anything and everything." Even with these expectations I don't think she realized that she was getting into . . . well, this:

241. At 8:00 a.m. on Thursday, the Voodoo Krewe masses at the Reynolds Club to prepare for their journey south to New Orleans. Space Cadet, the group's not so with-it navigator, is ready to go in his flight training uniform. The aptly named Aluminum Man may have a cold exterior immune to rust, but inside beats a tender heart. The Witch Doctoral Degree Candidate, clad in white lab coat and fully stocked with charms, trinkets, and talismans is ready for any harm that might befall the group. And then, of course, there's Prince. Far from their final forms, this motley Krewe of adepts—setting out in their Cajun-Style conveyance, the James Carville—will find much more than beads and beignets on their journey to the South: they will find themselves. [β points]

At 960 miles from Chicago, New Orleans would be the greatest distance of any of my four Scav Road Trips, even farther than the following year's trip to Toronto and Niagara Falls, and handily beating the jaunts to Minnesota and Iowa of the preceding two years. By way of List-required costume and, perhaps, personality, I was Space Cadet and wore a cape for the duration of the trip. My teammate Sean was the Witch Doctoral Candidate, Cullen was Prince, and Debbie was a metallic-leotard-clad Aluminum Man. The leotard was lent to her by a twenty-one-year-old intramural ballerina from Hitchcock and Debbie was further decorated in an emergency blanket cape and large sunglasses covered in aluminum foil. Debbie later mentioned that if she'd slept more than three hours the night before she might have never agreed to this outfit.

After getting fitted for our costumes, the four of us rested up for a few hours while the Road Trip coordinator, that year Edward Warden—a long-haired, voluble environmentalist— worked through the night, combing the List for Road Trip items and crafting an itinerary for us. This sublist, the bible of the Road Trip, is made of things the Judges saw along the way as they took the same road trip three weeks before. Road Trip coordinators on each team use Google Maps, intuition, and a lot of coffee to try to re-create the route the Judges took. These planners then create a map and list of addresses with driving time estimates and limiting factors like "When does the mustard museum close?" And they search for any teammates who have parents in whatever strange corners of America we may end up in, or, if that fails, make reservations at hotels with varying levels of cockroach infestation that meet the team's budgetary needs.

When we woke up on Thursday morning, Edward gave us our itinerary and we headed off into the unknown. Scav Road Trip is always weird and you always interact with some of the stranger parts of America. But Saturday of Road Trip 2013 got weirder than anything I've experienced before or since (even weirder than the Road Trip 2014 stop at the serial killer wax museum in Niagara Falls).

After bringing a banana, peanut butter, and hog jowl sandwich as an offering to Elvis Presley's grave site for item 188, and getting chased off the premises by a gargantuan and displeased security guard, we drove to Holly Springs, Mississippi. Here we found Graceland Too (as in "Graceland, also"—not "Graceland the second"), a twenty-four-hour Elvis museum run by a fanatically committed and clearly unstable fan named Paul McLeod. Our assignment was as follows:

201. Hey, you! Are you ready? Are you ready to offer Paul McLeod a flag of your choice to join the United Nation of Elvis Fans? Are you ready to examine the sustainable energy killing machine in his yard? Are you prepared to believe that he shot a beloved mythological creature? Are you prepared to leave by 10 a.m. at all costs? [3 points, 3 points, and 6 points, respectively]

As we followed Google Maps into a suburban neighborhood, we went from confused to concerned as Graceland Too appeared before us. It was a reasonably large two-story home on an otherwise quiet street, distinguished from its neighbors by having been painted not just one but two distinct shades of shocking blue seen mostly in screen savers and artwork purchased at Target. Its sidewalks were mounted with six-foot barbed wire fences and a smattering of American flags. Plastic blue conifers dotted the small yard, remnants of many cheap, fireproof Christmases long forgotten. The windows were blackened, painted over on the exterior, and the door ominously shut.

We could think of no worse idea than going inside this self-billed twenty-four-seven-three-sixty-five Elvis museum that looked like someone built to fidelity an eight-year-old's description of a nightmare. To our relief, another team pulled up then, our friendly rivals from the only slightly more aesthetically coherent complex known as Max Palevsky. We all agreed to go in together. Road Trip, unlike the competition on campus, requires a decent amount of collaboration, whether it be braving this Elvis museum, sharing directions in the middle of nowhere, or coordinating getting two cars out of a graveyard in rural Iowa. (And this wasn't BJ, so who cares.)

We rang the buzzer of Graceland Too to announce our arrival, then opened the door. We heard a bunch of noise coming from up a flight of stairs directly in front of us. There was chicken wire with black tarps behind it and a similar chicken-wire-covered gate at the top of the stairs. We heard varietal clanging noises emanating from above before Paul McLeod himself emerged, stringy-haired, clad in a rumpled polo shirt and a pair of unkempt khakis that looked like he was still working on buttoning them up.

So began the tour of Graceland Too, which looked more than anything like an Elvis-themed episode of *Hoarders*. McLeod led us into a room off the foyer with carpet that looked like it was from (and had last been cleaned in) the 1970s. There he turned on the disco ball for lighting and launched into an extensive, rambling speech about Elvis and his son, also Elvis. For four years after this event I thought McLeod was just referring to Elvis Presley as his—that is, McLeod's—metaphysical son, until an errant Google search led me to a

photo of Paul McLeod and his son, Elvis Aaron Presley Mc-
Leod, a separate human from the King.

McLeod's exaggerations were actually the subject of
item 227, which implored us to "remember the most fan-
tastical trivium they heard at Graceland Too?" for "2 'hundred thousand' points," mirroring Mr. McLeod's penchant
for stupendously large numbers to accentuate the details
of each of his factoids. Those ranged from claims that three
United States presidents, ABC, and NBC News had all visited Graceland Too, to a statement that he had once found
$100,000 in a car parked out behind his house along with
thirty-five Elvis suits. He even noted that Bill Clinton had
valued one of the albums in McLeod's collection at $250,000.
Most terrifyingly, McLeod specifically said, and I quote this
exactly because I still have the iPhone note I wrote in the
car after we left that day, "If I don't hang [your flag] up here
you can come back and cut my head off."

Key to this whole visit is that while three members of
our team were guys in our early twenties, our fearless leader-
slash-team mom Debbie was an adult woman in whom ole
Paul McLeod unfortunately took a particular interest. Paul
creepily followed her around his own labyrinthine home a
bit too closely. His disheveled manner, violent and bizarre
exaggerations, and low-budget Elvis extravaganza were already unsettling, but his leering, stalkerish pursuit of Debbie,
whom I had met literally three days before and mostly knew
as my friend's mom, was enough to convince me that this
was the closest I had ever come to being chained up in a
basement for the next few years of my life before meeting
my eventual demise due to my surely inadequate reverence
for the late Elvis Presley.

This impression was not at all dispelled as I proceeded
to what may once have been a dining room but was now
filled with the kind of cardboard trifolds you used for your

seventh grade science fair project on "how baseballs bounce differently when you put them in the oven," except for the fact that these trifolds featured Paul McLeod holding a wide variety of automatic weapons, as well as a strange series of photographs that McLeod explained was a record of a trip in which he and some other fans paid to go into a hotel room after Lisa Marie Presley, the daughter of Elvis, had stayed there but, importantly to them, *before* it had been cleaned. McLeod went into further detail, noting that they rolled around in the sheets that Lisa Marie had slept in, but not before trying to collect her pubic hair off the sheets.

Miraculously, things only got weirder as we progressed through rooms dimly lit by sparsely placed aging incandescent lights, including one red bulb attached to the nose of a taxidermied deer labeled Rudolf, the "mythological creature" of our Scav item.

A normal human would probably have turned back on the stoop, or after the decapitation joke, or almost certainly after the child's science project devoted to Paul McLeod's relationship with machine guns. But we were not normal humans at this point; we were Scavvies, and so we needed to finish the item, which in this case meant making it to the backyard to see the "sustainable energy killing machine." This turned out to be a homemade "electric chair" that was more of a poorly constructed wooden throne made of two-by-fours painted battleship gray with some wiring strewn about of the sort that is normally used in electric fences to corral cattle. After making a video of this ersatz execution machine, I shared some terrified eye contact and light jerks of the head with Cullen and Sean before making a swift exit along with our compatriots from Max P (and, I should be clear, Debbie, who was not left to her own fate at that particular residence).

Regrouped in our faithful minivan, we all sat there look-

ing at each other and saying some combination of "What just
happened?" before returning to our itinerary and navigating
toward the largest cedar bucket in Mississippi, then onward
to New Orleans, and Kentucky Stonehenge (which is exactly
what it sounds like), because Scav. We made it home safe
and sound, with points to earn and stories to tell.

Months later, Cullen would email all of us a news story
detailing how Paul McLeod had shot and killed a man on
his front porch before being found dead on that same porch
two days later. We didn't win Scav that year but we didn't
get shot inside a twenty-four-hour Elvis museum either, so
you win some and you lose some.

William Wilcox graduated in 2014 with a major in international studies and a minor in English and creative writing. He Scavved for Snell-
Hitchcock from 2011 to 2014, completing the Road Trip for the team all
four years. Originally from Warrenton, Virginia, William now lives in
Berkeley, California. William is currently completing a master's degree in
public policy at the University of California, Berkeley.

ROAD TRIP IS GREAT, CLEARLY, PROVIDED THAT YOU don't get taken hostage by an Elvis zealot with a homemade electric chair. But is it, perhaps, too commonplace, too played-out? What if you took the Road Trip and went one step further? In Scav, we are always looking to outdo ourselves. That's what Steven Lucy's essay is about . . .

ITEM 20:

SCAVAIR

Steven Lucy

2008 SCAV HUNT

Sometimes Scav items are very clear about what they're asking for. Sometimes, not so much.

20. Have your pre-selected Scav Warrior outside the Reynolds Club at 3:30 a.m. Thursday morning. They must be alone and they may not have any extraneous packages, bags or accessories. And, since it will be late into the evening, the attire for this event is evening-wear. Evening-wear with a bathing suit underneath. [α points]

Some prerequisites for this item had been coordinated before List Release: each team had preselected a Warrior, who had to comply with various criteria from able to "pitch a tent" and "recite the alphabet backwards" to having "a passable knowledge of the Board of Alcohol, Tobacco, Firearms and Explosives regulatory practices." They must "have seen the following movies: *Monty Python's Holy Grail, My Left Foot, Homeward Bound, Rain Man, 10,000 BC, Dirty Harry,* and *Thelma and Louise.*" They had to have a passport, not be needed in Chicago for the entirety of the Hunt, and submit to the Judges a list of allergies.

Each Warrior had also, two hours before List Release, submitted a duffel bag with clothing, a digital camera, an

ID, a credit card, three days' worth of cash, and a cell phone. Nothing else was allowed in the bags.

So at 3:30 a.m., just a few hours after List Release, at 57th and University, there were nine Scav Warriors in tuxes and evening gowns, ready for the unknown. Speculation had been rampant on team listhosts. Were they to be dropped in the forest? Taken to Canada? Manchuria? Was it all a hoax?

The Warriors were picked up in two cars. They were ceremoniously fed a spoonful of Jell-O. Pillowcases were placed over their heads. They were driven around for a while. And at 4:30 a.m., the pillowcases were removed.

Outside the car windows was a pre-dawn Midway Airport. Each Warrior was handed a boarding pass with their name on it. Destination: Las Vegas, Nevada.

* * *

The idea for ScavAir, the logical sequel to the Road Trip, had started quite some time earlier, and, depending on whom you ask, was either a running gag or a possible future item for many years.

You can trace its origins back to 2002, when an infamous item instructed Road Trip teams to leave room for the Prophet Elijah in their vehicles. A pair of items on the List completed the stunt:

312. At 8h00 on Friday, one non-Captain member of your team must arrive at 54th and Kimbark (don't get lost). They might want to bring $60 in personal burial money, a ripe orange, 15 sheets of lined paper (or a Big Chief tablet), one can of caffeine-free Coca Cola, two perfectly-glazed donuts, a valid U.S. passport, a plastic bag from Blockbuster Video, month-old menthol cigarettes, and a transcript reflecting a GPA of less than 2.5. That is all they can bring. Get your goodbyes out of the way beforehand. [510 points]

Scav members who reported to said corner at said time became abductees—sort of proto-Warriors, if you will—and were put on a bus to Ann Arbor, Michigan. Their cell phones were taken away and they were given a list of items to complete, including "Dead tired? Go to the funeral home and take a nap in a coffin" and "Nothin' says (safe) lovin' like a WWF condom." The final and highest-pointed item was to eat dinner at the Fleetwood Diner on Saturday night.

Meanwhile, the Road Trip had to complete this item:

117. Chill out, Mac! Between 20h00 and 21h00 on Saturday night, Mick and Lindsay are nowhere to be seen, but Chink and Chengwin take a break at the Fleetwood Diner in the hometown of the Wolverines to receive the next step nonetheless. And it's a doozy. [-1,500 points if Chunk and Chengwin do not complete this item]

Over dinner in Ann Arbor, each abductee was united with their respective Road Trip team and given a ride home to Chicago.

Two years later, in 2004, the Judges requested that each team provide the names of three members—at least one male and one female, and at least one over twenty-one—who were ready to be gone from Chicago for the whole Hunt. People suspected ScavAir as the natural next step. But this turned out to be a complete misdirect: these brave Scavvies were sent nowhere at all.

In 2005 the Judges had discussed sending the Road Trip to Toronto and from there flying one member of each Road Trip team to Iqaluit, Nunavut, in the far remote reaches of northern Canada, which sees a daily average high of 18 degrees Fahrenheit in May. This was eventually ruled out as cost-prohibitive, with round-trip flights running $3,200 a pop.

Other destinations were also discussed (Seattle, Tijuana, Miami, Los Angeles, a random Caribbean island), but the plan never got further than a prank email "accidentally" leaked to the captains listhost. Scavvies scrambled to prepare, but, again, no ScavAir took place.

ScavAir was becoming the kind of hoax that teams were expecting, and they were no longer taking the bait. So, of course, that meant it was the perfect time to actually do it.

After Scavving for three teams and then judging for two years, I graduated in 2006. As time marched on toward 3:30 a.m. on the Thursday before Mother's Day 2008, I was living in New York City, leading a generally responsible adult life, no longer active in Scav planning. I was in the postcollege "career searching" phase of life, and most of my income came from writing boring software for boring people with boring business plans.

Then a call came out over the Judges listhost: would any former Judges like to organize some items in Las Vegas?

The current active Judges had somehow wrangled a few thousand dollars out of Student Government to pull off the ScavAir stunt, but they still had a very tight budget and were in need of logistical support, since none of the active Judges wanted to miss the Hunt in Chicago.

I was intrigued. Running a scavenger hunt for four days was definitely more interesting than writing boring software. But my first reaction was that I was being pranked. "All right, Jim, give me the low-down," I wrote to Head Judge Jim Ryan. "Is this yet another rendition of an old prank, or do I actually need to clear my schedule in May?" He assured me it was legit, and so I bought my plane ticket. Sebastian Ellefson and Courtney Prokopas, two other recently retired Judges, were also on board, and about thirty-six hours before List Release took place in Ida Noyes, we got on planes to Vegas, with no budget, a reservation for two hotel rooms, and no list.

* * *

Upon landing in Sin City on Thursday morning, each of the

Warriors received a text message from a mysterious phone number telling them that a limo was waiting. Past security on the arrivals level, they found a driver with a sign reading "Scav Hunt." They followed him. A short limo drive up the Strip brought them to the Stratosphere Hotel, where the driver dropped off the Scavvies with instructions to head to the pool.

At the pool, in the midmorning desert sun, they found Courtney, Sebastian, and me waiting for them, wearing Judge shirts that had been hastily FedExed from Chicago. Floating in an inner tube in the middle of the pool was Courtney, holding a stack of Lists that we had printed less than an hour earlier in the hotel business center. The Scavvies stripped off their tuxedos and ball gowns until they were down to their swimwear and then jumped in to swim after Courtney. That was our List Release, Vegas edition.

The Occidental Judges, as we styled ourselves, had arrived in Vegas Tuesday night, and on Wednesday we had written a List for Thursday, as well as arranging for the limousine that met the Scavvies at the airport and a few other logistical details. It was the full brainstorm-cut-edit-typeset-print process that takes place over months for regular Scav, but compressed into one day.

In addition to giving the Scavvies their own List Release, we tried to re-create other Scav touchstones. The List was typeset in the usual format, using LaTeX. The rules were full of in-jokes. The first item was, as is traditional, just a copy of the main Scav Hunt List (that much harder without access to campus printers and team HQ). We had our own Vegas Scavenfeast at the cheapest buffet we could find. There was an Occidental Judgment on Saturday morning, after which we would head to the airport to make it back in time for Oriental Judgment on Sunday.

Other items ranged from "be a witness at a wedding"

to "find a New Yorker in the New York, New York casino" to "inclinate to the highest floor" (the angled elevator in the Luxor Hotel, styled an "inclinator," would only operate to the floor programmed into your room key card, so this was an exercise in tailgating or sweet-talking). We sent them to do tacky Vegas things and to go off the beaten path, to anonymous commercial streets and government buildings. And we Judges learned some important lessons—for example, walking slowly around a casino, not gambling, while taking notes will get you a not-optional interview with security real fast. We even somehow convinced Penn and Teller to be the audience for some dumb Scavvie magic tricks. (The Warriors told P and T they would make themselves disappear—and then ran out of the room. I think Penn and Teller were genuinely surprised by how bad the trick was.)

The nine Scavvies all stayed in one hotel room. But the Ann Arbor bus abductees of 2002 had spent the night in an ATM vestibule, so we figured we were showing some serious generosity.

Although the Judges had convinced the U of C administration to provide funding to fly nine unsuspecting students to an undisclosed location, we somehow hadn't succeeded in convincing the university to give money for the students to gamble. So all of the Judges chipped in and we came up with a couple hundred bucks of personal donations, which we divided among our Warriors. Each Scavvie was given $20 and we allotted one hour to gamble as much as they wanted; they got to keep the proceeds *and* got one real Scav point per dollar won. Most of them went bust and got 0 points, though a few Scavvies made out handsomely.

That last morning in Vegas, when we gathered around the pool for Occidental Judgment, we ran into a problem we hadn't anticipated: Though the nine Warriors were nominally representing different teams, they'd stuck together for most of the sixty or so hours they were in Vegas. They had all become fast friends through shared experience and no longer saw each other as competitors. This made Occidental Judgment anticlimactic, as most items were completed by either everyone or no one. In the end, the gambling item produced the largest point differential, which I suppose is fitting. KPM of the FIST, who won over $80 at the roulette table, came out as the official winner of ScavAir.

But all of our Warriors had done something remarkable, I reflected after the twelve of us flew to Chicago so we could be there for Oriental Judgment on Sunday. There we saw the massive teams present their items with the help of databases, page captains, five-digit budgets, and decked-out HQs, and this made me appreciate our Warriors all the more. They had volunteered to go into the unknown, found themselves in a strange city with no support structure and with their teams relying on them, and had thrown themselves into their task body, mind, and spirit. And as for me—well, even though I was technically an adult, I had done something a lot more valuable than writing boring software for boring people with boring business plans.

Steven Lucy discovered Scav Hunt in the worst way possible: with the disaster List Release of 2003 ("the List is buried somewhere on the lakefront"). For some reason he stuck around and Scavved for Pierce, helped re-found the Breckinridge team, and joined the FIST before eventually becoming a Judge in 2005. After graduating in 2006 with degrees in mathematics and the history, philosophy, and social studies of science and medicine, he wrote boring software for a few years and now runs Open Produce, Cornell Florist, and 57th Street Wines in the Hyde Park neighborhood of Chicago.

WHEN THE OCCIDENTAL JUDGES TRIED TO RE-CREATE AS
many Scav touchstones as possible in Las Vegas, they naturally
had to get some wordplay in there. What, after all, is a Scav List
without some dumb puns? The Vegas Judges came up with this:
"Do your best flamingo imbirdination. We should only just be able
to pick you out from the flock of live, shrimp-eating water fowl."
Imbirdination is pretty good. But it's got nothing on some of these
puntastic gems from years past . . .

30 PUN ITEMS

1998.347: A white snake, a quiet riot, a warrant, some poison, and a motley crew. [3 points per item. 10 bonus points for a deaf leopard]

2001.113: Scabhunt 2001. [3 points per fully formed and dried scab, attached to a person, 20 scabs maximum]

2002.020: The Moulin Luge . . . Costumes required . . . [85 points for farthest slid using only pure inertia, 70 points for second-farthest, 50 points for third-farthest]

2002.59: You know how a fire hydrant has water in it? We want a water hydrant. [83 points]

2003.1: *The Comma Sutra.* Prepare positions for all punctuation! [22.3 points]

2003.46: Möbius stripper. Must be non-orientable. Must not emphasize the one-dimensionality of the stripper's personality. [28 points]

2004.17: Mandelbrotwurst. [17 points]

2004.53: Is that a keg in your pants, 'cause I wanna tap that ass. No really, I do. Must be fully functional as both pants and a keg holder. [54 points]

2004.66: A G-string string quartet rendition of this year's theme song. [4 × 9.7 points]

2005.203: A Will to Power Bar [2 points]

2005.260: Mai-Tai kickboxing. [0.25 points]

2005.261: Blintzkrieg. [0.25 points]

2005.264: BroccoLiam Neeson. [0.25 points]

> The previous three items were from an entire page
> of low-scoring food-based pun items supposedly
> written by fictitious judge "Will Westin."

2006.3: Garden Gnome Chomsky. [3 points]

2006.49: Chumbawumba bop bags. Must play "Tubthumping." [10 points]

> They get knocked down, but they get up again. You
> ain't ever gonna keep them down.

2006.80: Marzipander to our marziphantasies! Your marzipanoramic marzipanoply should include marzipansies, a marzipanzer, marziPeter Pan, a marzipanda, a marzipangolin, a marziPan paniscus, marzipanpipes, a marzipancreas, a marzipanther, and marzipots and pans, but should by no means create marzipandemonium. Presenter must be suitably attired in marzipants. [23 points]

2007.71: A Gingerbread House of Ill Repute. [16 points]

2007.191: How much bacca could a Chewbacca chew if a Chewbacca could chew bacca? [8 points]

2008.63: A Helen or rose of felt. [1 point] A nancy's ray gun. [2 points] A ladybird's johnson. [3 points]

2009.67: Why do you cherish that tea cosy so much, mother? I daresay you love it even more than your own daughter. It's just an old tea cosy, mother. It's just a ratty old Mr. T cosy . . . [7 points]

2011.27: A simple loaf of bread made with flour, water, and Yeats. [2 points]

2011.121: A rust belt. A Bible belt. A borscht belt. [3 points]

2012.295: The appropriate music video for "I'm Bringing Skeksi Back". [6 points]

> Skeksis are the reptilian birdlike race from *The Dark Crystal*. Not that having that piece of knowledge made the videos presented for this item any more explicable.

2014a.252: Why isn't there a comprehensive Wild Wild West wiki? Ideally called "Wiki Wild Wild West." Wiki wiki wild. Wiki wild. Wiki wild wild west. Like all good wikis, collaboration is encouraged. [3 points]

2014b.6: Max Weber Grillz. [1 point]

2014b.94: Magic 8-Balls are too polite. Bring us a Magic Hate-Ball. [12 points]

2014b.224: A Shaq-in-the-box, Shaq'o'Lantern, and battleShaqxe. [3 points each, and that's a fact]

2015.3: Is your refrigerator running? THEN YOU'D BETTER CANVAS FOR IT! SHOW YOUR SUPPORT, AND HELP IT GET ELECTED! [5 points; 2 extra points for the "winner"]

> A surprisingly beloved item, chants of "FRIDGE FOR YOU! FRIDGE FOR ME! F-G-H-1-9-6-P!" (the model number of a team's minifridge) would be heard throughout the weekend. And also 2016. It was that kind of election.

2016.46: A Jar Jar jar, ajar Jar Jar [4 points]

2017.169: An Eric Carle Marx collage-print book, perfect for your darling proletariat infants! [24 points]

EVEN WHEN YOU'RE NOT ON ROAD TRIP, OR FLYING blindfolded to Las Vegas, travel can play a big role in Scav. In 2005, I was studying abroad in England for the year, and I made the executive decision to spend roughly all my savings and skip two days of classes to fly to Chicago for the Hunt. I felt pretty proud of my dedication to Scav . . . until I talked to a Judge who had come in all the way from China.

Even when they can't be in Chicago over Mother's Day weekend, the truly dedicated find a way to be involved no matter where in the world they are.

ITEM 293:

WHERE THERE IS NO DUCT TAPE

Erica Pohnan
2015 SCAV HUNT

What is it like to do Scav Hunt from Indonesia? Well, listen up, friends. You get the List during lunch break, there is no Home Depot so you mostly need to build things using bamboo and machetes, and DUCT TAPE DOESN'T WORK. This is thanks to that disaster we call 100 percent humidity, and grade F duct tape from China. During the 2015 Hunt, I was forced to break up with duct tape and switch to zip ties, and I am never looking back.

From 2013 to 2016, I lived and worked in rural Borneo, Indonesia. Across the street from my house was a huge jungle full of wild orangutans and hornbills, and I used to wake up every morning to the sound of gibbons singing. Day-to-day life working for a health and environmental conservation NGO was not too dissimilar from normal Scav Hunt ("Everyone drop what you're doing now and help us put out this forest fire / catch this runaway cow / save the life of this motorcycle crash victim"), but I still missed and craved Chicago in May, that four-day break from the ordinary to build trebuchets, learn choreographed dances, and admire the creative ways that my fellow Scavvies had devised to zip-line watermelons across the quads. The problem is that

Scav Hunt in Chicago was a five-hour speedboat ride, and then about thirty-six hours of plane rides, away.

Which is how I found myself scanning the 2015 List, trying to identify every item that I could do all the way from the jungles of Borneo. And I found one.

293. Hypnotizing a chicken seems easy, but if the Wikipedia article on the practice is to be believed, debate on the optimal method is heated. Do some trials on a real chicken and submit a report . . . for science of course. [4 piece points]

I thought, "Aha! If I were a Scavvie in Chicago I would be tearing my hair out trying to figure out how to acquire a chicken. But not here in West Kalimantan, in this small town that is drowning in chickens." And it is true, many other teams did this item successfully. But it probably took them more than ten minutes to find a chicken, and they probably did not acquire a feisty, Borneo-bred village chicken the likes of which I purchased from my housekeeper Rena for about $6.

Rena and I bound the chicken into a box, and I drove down the road to the beach where a group of my Indonesian colleagues had casually gathered to enjoy the spectacle of a foreigner running around, trying and failing to hypnotize a chicken.

Three volunteers helped with video recording, scientific note-taking, and chicken wrangling, should the subject attempt to escape. We dutifully tested all three methods of chicken hypnotization detailed on Wikipedia. The first method (drawing a line in the sand with a stick away from the chicken's beak) and the third method (cradling the chicken in your arms until it fell asleep) failed utterly and made me very grateful for the chicken wranglers.

Do you know how fast chickens can run? Believe me,

friends, as I later learned, once they escape, they are gone forever.

The second method, which I nicknamed "The Wattle to Vent Violation Method" (i.e., laying a chicken on its back and stroking it gently until it calmed down), absolutely succeeded, much to the delight of the crowd. We hypnotized our chicken for a full one minute and forty seconds before it snapped out of its trance and attempted to escape.

For days afterward, I was approached by my Indonesian colleagues saying, "Wow! I had no idea you could do that!" Their statements amazed me, as I had assumed they were full of their own traditional, indigenous secrets for managing the mischief of chickens. I had not expected to be able to show anything new to a town of farming families where everyone and their mother-in-law has a chicken coop behind their house.

Hypnotizing that chicken was a new kind of Scav victory. Sure, it's fun when Scav forces you to acquire new skills like electromagnetic aeolian harp construction or blindfolded square dance performance on roller skates just to complete an item. But it's also incredibly gratifying when an item is easy to do just because it's part of your ordinary life.

This is one of the reasons why I still Scav, now more than ten years postgraduation. I am still waiting for that one-in-a-million item worth 300 points that you happen to have stowed away in the family attic—but that nobody else on earth can do. Snitchcock will move heaven and earth spending infinite resources and time to get it done, Max P will fake it with duct tape and cardboard, and GASH will replace it with a giant statue of Bender from Futurama that can catapult tacos into a Judge's mouth and tell the Judge that this is what they actually wanted instead of the original item. And you will just have it right there and waiting for you. The 2015 Hunt was the closest I've ever come to that one-in-a-million moment.

Not everything I did for that Hunt was as much of a success. I also tried my hand at item 213, "A hoop skirt that makes Heffernen's Booty come to life [18 points]." This item refers to a highly disturbing painting that depicts a naked woman wearing a hoop skirt made of dead animals. I was wandering through the jungle behind my office, gathering foliage to be used as decorative ornamentation for the Heffernen's Booty with live animals (I had further plans for that chicken), when I ran into an illegal logger dragging a bundle of three-meter-long trees behind him. We both froze when we saw each other. In my head I thought, "Aha, caught! So you illegally log on Sundays when no one is working?!" And he probably thought, "Why did this girl gather so many plants that are secretly covered in fire ants?"

These are both valid questions, which failed to mitigate the supreme awkwardness of accidentally confronting an illegal logger in the midst of a technically criminal act while I did an item incorrectly and got covered in fire ants in the process. Honestly, it was nowhere near my most awkward Scav moment, nor the most incorrectly I have ever done an item, nor the weirdest look I have gotten during Scav. But it *was* the first time I had to forage in the jungle to complete an item, which I can't imagine many other Scavvies have done.

You may wonder what ultimately became of the chicken. Obviously, we used him again in item 304: "Why don't you tell that chicken from item 293 what Werner Herzog really thinks about it! [1 point]" The chicken's reaction was later described in the research report as "An artless attempt to appear contemptuously unconcerned while its frequent eye blinking betrayed the hurt within."

His duties fulfilled, I released him behind my house

the next morning. He exploded out of the box in a flurry of
feathers and immediately started chasing after my neighbor's roosters, obeying his basic chicken instincts to murder
them all. I never saw him again, but I assume that he joined
my neighbor's chicken flock—dutifully waking me up at 2
a.m., 3 a.m., 4 a.m. with his incessant crowing, exacting his
revenge every night for all the years I lived in Indonesia.

Erica Pohnan graduated in 2007, after Scavving for Max Palevsky from
2004 to 2008 and cocaptaining the winning 2005 team "Team Fluffy: Destroyer of Worlds." As an environmental studies major, postgraduate work
took her to undertake forest conservation work in faraway places from
which she occasionally made it back to Chicago (or not) to Scav for GASH
from 2011 to 2015. She currently works for the United Nations in Bangkok.

SURPRISINGLY, NONE OF THE ITEMS THAT ERICA POHNAN describes in her essay are my favorite Scav use for chicken. That honor belongs to this item from the 2008 Scav Olympics:

02. Cockfighting! At last! Except cockfighting is terribly inhumane and often results in the death of the bird. But you can't kill something that's already dead! As such, prepare your marionette-whole-roaster-chicken-fighters for battle. We will strap bags of giblets on them (BYOGiblets) and you must use your warrior fowl's razor spurs to spill the entrails of your opponent onto the thirsty ground. Experts recommend using the Mexican straight blade for a quicker and cleaner kill. The Filipino curved blade is just cruel.

Picture artful puppetry of bird carcasses, as they nimbly jab their razor-blade-covered wings at one another. Now picture what *actually* happened, which was Scavvies wildly swinging around frozen rotisserie chickens with knives strapped to them, with every parry nearly stabbing a competitor in the knee or the groin. The rest of us stood in a tight circle around the puppeteers and alternately cheered them on or leapt backward in terror as their armed chickens swung in our direction. It was one of the funniest things I've ever seen, only because I did not get stabbed. I wish every supermarket chicken came ready for a knife fight.

Here are some other undignified items that have happened to animals both living and dead over the years.

14 ITEMS THAT ANIMALS
COULD HAVE DONE WITHOUT

1988.151: A live piglet (please on a leash or restrained in some manner). [50 points]

1991.75: A person milking a live cow: bring a pail, a stool, and the cow. (all or nothing, and don't forget the bovine) [261 points]

1993.153: A flock of live sheep (3 or more) with a fraternity member as a shepherd. [150 points + 15 bonus points if aforementioned shepherd is grinning and holding the items in 1993.60]

> 1993.60 asked for "Condoms in all the colors of the rainbow."

1997.46: A large stuffed monkey in riot gear; be sure to include helmet with faceplate, plexi-glass shield, bullet-proof vest, and night stick [36 points, 200 points for a real live monkey—no lemurs!]

> A real, live, adorable monkey was indeed present on the college quads during the 1997 Hunt. However, it was somewhat overshadowed by . . .

1997.106: A real, live, breathing elephant. [500 points]

> This happened. We have photos to prove it.

1998.02: The Great Squirrel Summon. To be held on the Main Quads Saturday at 3pm. Each team will mark out one 10' x 10' area and must bring own equipment to measure and mark area. Clean up afterwards is mandatory, and teams may not injure any person or animal. Squirrel calls and pheromones may be used, but no restraining devices. [5 points per squirrel within the region during Judge's passing by]

> The University of Chicago is known for its squirrel population. A popular campus T-shirt once proclaimed that they were "prettier than the girls and more aggressive than the guys." This T-shirt was heteronormative but accurate.

2004.230: Plastinate a tilapia. Plastinate it real good. Pointing will be based both on effectiveness of the plastination process and presentation of the end result. [20 points]

> Inspired by the Body Worlds exhibit that was then making its home at the Museum of Science and Industry.

2010.42: Maybe we wouldn't be the school "where the squirrels are more aggressive than the guys" if we had more diurnal raptors around. Get a fully-trained NAFA member to show his stuff on campus. [37 points]

> NAFA being the North American Falconers Association. The fellow Max Palevsky brought in was hoping the opportunity would gain support for his admittance into the law school. The Judges signed his petition, as it's hard to say no to a guy with a diurnal raptor clenched to his arm.

2011.51: A basketball hoop that's a rib cage. A RIB CAGE! [12 points]

> For this item, a reference to a Tracy Jordan monologue from *30 Rock*, it was thought that teams would use ribs that one could acquire at one of the many Hyde Park BBQ restaurants. Not so for the MacPierce

team, who went ahead and dragged a road-killed deer carcass back with them from the road trip, cut out its ribcage, then bleached it.

2011.256: A lion, tiger, or bear. With trainer. On campus. [125 points, 25 bonus points if it does a trick the assembled Judges deem "righteous"]

Sadly, unlike the free-range elephants of yore, the school administration required these majestic beasts to be confined to cages on the Midway Plaisance. On the other hand, if the biggest problem you have during a Scav Hunt is that you're required to keep the large carnivorous beasts in cages, things must be going pretty well.

2012.02: A reverse dog sled race. Dog must remain on sled solely through its own free will. Sleds that lose their dogs will be disqualified.

2012.290: Ain't no rule says a dog can't play *Space Invaders*™! In fact, this item requires that your dog play *Space Invaders*. Your dog may, and should, use a modified gaming system, but aside from setting up and accessing the playable screen, no human intervention is allowed. Modded systems should not change how *Space Invaders*™ the game actually functions. [30 points. 5 extra points for the top dog]

Most completions involved coating a game controller with peanut butter. And were adorable.

2014.262: A tiny fiddler crab. Must possess tiny fiddle. [6 points]

2017.77: Kitty keeps napping on my keyboard. I think he wants attention, so let's show kits on stream! GIVE 🐱 your own ResidentSleeper a Twitch channel and allow it to make meaningful contributions to gameplay via feline input devices. [18 points, with c4t bonus points if it can flame chat! As always, rule 6's "no harming animals" clause applies.]

> Yes, there is a rule in the official Scav Hunt rule book that forbids hurting animals. You'd think this could go without saying, but you'd also think dead moose could just be left alone, so clearly it never hurts to make these expectations explicit.

AS I MENTIONED IN THIS BOOK'S INTRODUCTION, THE University of Chicago is kind of famous for not knowing how to have fun. In 2010, we made the *Huffington Post*'s list of "the top ten anti-party schools," and we took that as a point of pride.

But during Scav Hunt, things are different. Sure, the culture is every bit as nerdy and focused as it is the other 361 days of the year—probably even more so. But for once, the focus is on *frivolity*. Students emerge from the library. They interact with strangers. They even—yes, it's true—party.

But this is not a natural state of being for everyone. Some of them need some prompting. And that's where this next essay comes in.

ITEM 238:

WE LIKE TO PARTY

Moacir P. de Sá Pereira

SCAV HUNT

When I started doing the Hunt, I was disappointed to find it pretty isolating. Though touted in orientation materials as an opportunity for engaged and sustained freak flag flying, for me the Hunt was no different than doing homework. I'd sit in my team's central command and fold origami cranes for hours or search for answers on AltaVista. I don't think I even showed up to Judgment those first two years.

Teams had networks of belonging within them, but nothing bound teams to other teams. Similarly, little bound the Hunt to the larger university community. As the other essays in this collection show, lots of very creative work was emerging from the Scavvies' efforts, but at the time, the audience was punishingly small.

Having a distant adjudicator assess the results of your freaking out for four days to complete a task that would vanish into thin air afterward described both working for the Hunt and writing a Hum paper.[1] I take that back; the idea of spending four days on a Hum paper is inconceivable. So the Hunt reproduced the pedagogical isolation of the university, as well. Aspects of the Hunt that contribute to

---

1. "Hum" refers to "Humanities," which, along with "Sosc" (short for "Social Sciences"), comprises part of the U of C's Core curriculum.

its aura, like how Scavvies bring *the same level* of devotion and energy to the Hunt that they do their coursework, also have a flip side, where the Hunt itself gives *the same level* of dissatisfaction and invalidation as a five-page essay read by only one person does.

In short, what was touted as the biggest scavenger hunt in the world never felt like it.

So when I became a Judge, I didn't just want to write items—I was there to change the culture. The Hunt as a whole was a community, I believed, and I'd prove it. Those freak flags were going to fly high and proud.

The idea I had—and I don't claim sole authorship because, like, twenty years—was to distribute Judgment throughout the entire Hunt. Instead of just building *objects* that were impressive in their detail, teams would also have to orchestrate *events* that would be impressive in their detail. Teams would see one another during the course of the Hunt and sometimes would even have to work together.

Similarly, Judges would become publicly available. We would be involved in the activities, recognizable in our Judge T-shirts. Earlier Hunts would dock teams if noncaptains spoke to Judges. But in the late 1990s, we shifted the role of Judge from distant cleric to hands-on mediator. The explicit goal now was to make *everyone* know that the Hunt was on, thereby making everyone feel like they had some stake in the Hunt.

To encourage this, the 1999 Hunt was the first to have a schedule that featured events on every day, from what I believe was the first stage-managed List Release all the way through to Judgment. We introduced the first quad item that year:

213. Your own _____-In on the Quads, beginning Thursday at noon, ending at 3:00 pm. Must include team members forcing themselves to have _____, as well as administrators who disapprove of the _____. [178 points]

A reference to the contemporaneous on-campus protest of the lack of a women's center, this item both supported (obliquely) the protest and mocked it. But more than anything, it was there on the quads to engage the normies who were just trying to get to class. We hoped that events like the _____-in would get more people excited about the Hunt and integrate it more deeply into the rhythms of the university. Furthermore, now required to produce and perform throughout, teams could no longer hide until Judgment.

The big show, though, would be Saturday night:

338. The Vengabus is coming / And everybody's jumping / New York to San Francisco / An intercity disco / The wheels of steel are turning / And traffic lights are burning / So if you like to party / Get on and move your body. Saturday night, parking lot TBA. BYOBus and make it good. [600 points maximum]

And let me tell you, the party the Scavvies threw would have made the Venga Boys proud. Shoreland got a school bus and filled it with first years, including some jumping up and down on the bus's roof. BJ's bus was a conversion van, and then there were several variations on the theme in between. Somehow we managed to secure the center of the quads as the "parking lot" mentioned in the item, and a tradition was born.

The "Party on the Quads" became the non-Judgment centerpiece of the Hunt. DJs with quad-shaking sound systems became de rigueur. Alcohol-and-etc.-related content soared alongside. Everything was free, everything was available. As one chronicler might have said, "Bliss was it in that dawn to be alive, but to be young was very heaven!" Teams mingled, and even non-Scavvies started looking forward and coming to the party.

On the one hand, hooray! Lots of people were getting

excited about the Hunt and having fun in ways not micro-managed by the administration. On the other hand, this meant that sometimes things could get . . . out of hand. One year, our staff advisor was drenched by a Super Soaker (filled with water, I hope), and it took some effort to convince her that she was not intentionally targeted and there was no reason to shut everything down. There were kiddie pools, fake volcanoes, and lots of nudity, near-nudity, and threats of further nudity. We, by which I mean I, told ourselves that these parties were perfectly "legal," because the quads were university property. Feeding alcohol to minors on private property is allowed, right? Didn't Milton Friedman die for that right or something?

I imagine that the event items may have sometimes felt like a huge weight, dragging teams away from building their electric guitars that spit fire or whatever. But, honestly, a singular focus on a singular task isn't healthy; recall the idea of spending four days on a Hum paper above. Forcing yourself to go to the quads, get naked, and drink Jell-O shots with the person from your Sosc class who insisted every Tuesday and Thursday like clockwork that everything was about taking over the means of production isn't, really, that bad.

In 2003, I became a Very Serious Grad Student and left the Hunt behind. But by then, Scav had given me the sense of community and belonging that I'd always hoped it would. And in return, I gave Scav a party that helped define it.

Moacir P. de Sá Pereira teaches in the English Department at New York University, where he studies how objects form communities in the spaces within novels. In 1998, he unilaterally decided to use the typesetting software LaTeX to format the List, a tradition that persists to this day.

ALL GOOD THINGS MUST COME TO AN END. FLY TOO close to the sun, and you're going to get burned. Add in your own aphorism here. The point is that the outrageous parties that Moacir P. de Sá Pereira described in the last essay had to go somewhere. And here's where they went.

ITEM 47:

A PARTY AT THE END OF DAYS

Dave Franklin

2006 SCAV HUNT

"Time counts and keeps countin', and we knows now finding the trick of what's been and lost ain't no easy ride. But that's our trek, we gotta travel it. And there ain't nobody knows where it's gonna lead. Still in all, every night we does the tell, so that we 'member who we was and where we came from . . ."

—Savannah Nix, *Mad Max: Beyond Thunderdome*

The wind on Friday afternoon was around a six on the Beaufort wind force scale, a "strong breeze" that, coupled with thirty-eight-degree temperatures and the threat of snow, made it feel more like March than May. There's a reason why unsanctioned T-shirts proclaim the U of C to be "proof that Hell does freeze over." As my teammates and I lay the groundwork for what we envisioned to be a grand outdoor Thunderdome, the wind whipped at my cape and tore away our building supplies, and I wondered how the hell we were going to make this Party work.

The Friday night Party, deserving of capitalization for its legend of annual excess, always happened at the center of the university's main quad. Every team set up thematically decorated enclosures that hid vast quantities of alcohol within. The school administration trusted everyone involved to comport themselves with something like dignity. This trust was unearned, but I guess the best I can say is that we hadn't yet proven how much we didn't deserve it.

The Party mattered a lot, but my team, Max Palevsky, was notoriously bad at it. Our Party sucked and everyone knew it. So when Jonathan Williams and I were elevated to team captains for the 2006 Hunt, we vowed to make the Party a Priority. We showed up to the Captains' Breakfast on Thursday morning, where we and all the other captains were, in accordance with item 260, dressed up as Quailman from the animated TV show *Doug*. (If you ever want to make this outfit for yourself, all it requires is: [1] a headband made out of a belt, [2] a cape made out of a towel, and [3] wearing your underwear on the outside of your pants.) And that's when we learned what kind of party we were in for.

47. All Tomorrow's Parties. In the not too distant future, next Friday AD, the teams will host a shindig, to the delight of you and me. Stop arguing over whether the future will be a totalitarian government dystopia or a privatized corporate dystopia and head on over to the quads for a blast from the, er, opposite of past. To help you answer the immortal question, "Whatever happened to the parties of tomorrow?", individual "Visions . . . of . . . the Future!" will be given out at Scav Captains and the Meeting of Tomorrow. The future's so bright, we're gonna need shades. [Δ points]

The individual Vision . . . of . . . the Future we were assigned was *Mad Max: Beyond Thunderdome*, the underrated third installment of the *Mad Max* film franchise. Starring Tina Turner as "Aunty Entity," the ruler of Bartertown, the film features the Thunderdome, a gladiator arena–cum–justice system. So on Friday afternoon, we went to the quad to construct our own Thunderdome, which would double as an alcohol enclosure and as an actual (but probably safe) fighting arena.

But Beaufort's winds just got stronger as the temperature continued to drop, and the idea of an outdoor party started to seem not only unpleasant but possibly dangerous. No one had prepared for a Mother's Day weekend snowstorm, so Head Judge Courtney had frantic last-minute negotiations with the administration, and at the eleventh hour they came to the completely insane conclusion that the party should be moved indoors—into, of all places, Cobb Lecture Hall.

Cobb is, according to Wikipedia, the "first and most expensive of the campus's original sixteen buildings. Constructed in 1892, it was modeled after Gothic buildings at University of Oxford." And if you can't trust an expensive old classroom building in the hands of hundreds of drunk, sleep-deprived college undergrads led by some people wearing underwear on top of their pants, who *can* you trust?

But Scav Hunt is important, the Party's a Scav cornerstone, and staying outdoors would be a fast track to hypothermia. Cobb seemed like the best choice. And so we took our building materials inside to transmogrify a classroom on the fifth floor of Cobb into a postapocalyptic hellscape.

After an hour of frenzied interior design, our classroom was ringed with chicken wire and festooned with aesthetically pleasing trash. We scrawled "THUNDERDOME" on the whiteboard, blared menacing yet danceable music on the sound system, and nestled alcoholic beverages into their required hiding places.

Word had spread throughout the student body that the Scav Party was now in Cobb, and many more people than usual turned up for the chance to let loose in the rooms where they had, perhaps, struggled through *The Wealth of Nations*, hoping to both grasp and ultimately evade the invisible hand of poor decision-making. Usually the Scav Party was seen as a little weird, or at least niche—people who liked to spend their nights playing beer pong in the basement of Alpha Delt generally weren't turning up for the Scav Party.

But tonight, they were. Tonight, no matter who you were, the Scav Party was *the* party.

Now, due to sleep deprivation and some alcohol consumption, my memory of the evening is somewhat corrupted, missing a time-stamped progression of events and rendered as a hazy, much less sexy scene cut from *Eyes Wide Shut*. I remember fellow students surging through the halls on five floors, the Scavvies among them dressed in every sort of futuristic costume. I could tell that people were drinking a lot—maybe *too* much, the future responsible adult in me thought.

After a quick circuit of the other teams' subparties—all of which appeared to be quite epic—I returned to the Thunderdome and was accosted by a teammate yelling, "Can we goat wrestle?!" Not knowing what that was, but determined to be the captain that my team needed, I said, "Yes!" A new ring of chicken wire was assembled and individuals proceeded to drunkenly "goat wrestle," which involved getting on hands and knees and, using heads only, attempting to flip opponents onto their backs. The gathered crowd roared with delight, chanting, "Two men enter! One man leaves!," a line that makes perfect sense both in *Mad Max: Beyond Thunderdome* and also in a Western civilization classroom. This chant became part of the Scav lexicon for years to come. Max Palevksy had finally thrown a fun party.

Stories started filtering through the building, however. People were urinating in the corners of classrooms. Some were absconding into the night with chairs and desks. The Party was just this side of completely out of control, without a clear presence of authority, no Aunty Entity keeping the peace. At some point, an actual member of the university staff saw what was going down and frantically told the Judges that they needed to shut it down *now*. The Judges stormed through the classrooms, turning off sound systems and turning on lights, and the non-Scavvies fled like cockroaches, leaving the Scavvies to clean up the mess, which we did, I think.

The next morning, Scav Hunt charged on, and it wasn't until the next year that we fully understood how much we had destroyed. The following year, the party, now decapitalized, became a tamer affair, regulated tightly by the university with limited drink tickets and security screenings. After that, Scav pretty much stopped having Friday night parties entirely. Better to have nothing, many felt, than pathetic reminders of the glory that once was.

The 2006 Party was meant to be a collection of the parties of the future, only to become fossilized as the final Party of Scav Hunts Past. While I am sorry that we ruined the Party for future generations, I also know that you can't have a post-apocalypse without an apocalypse. The Party of 2006 was ours. And maybe through the telling here, *we can 'member who we was and where we came from.*

Dave Franklin (AB '08) majored in cinema and media studies and English language and literature. After two years on the Max Palevsky team (2005–2006), Dave took a year off from active hunting to make his feature-length student documentary *Scavengers* (2007). He then joined the Snell-Hitchcock team for two more hunts (2008–2009). Dave now lives in New York City, working as a distributor of international classic cinema and occasionally writing.

SOME SCAV ITEMS ARE FUNNY IN THEIR OWN RIGHT

(e.g., "sorry about the syphilis, can we still be cousins?") and can be traced back no further than an in-joke that once amused the Judges. Other items are riffs on memes or cultural phenomena (like the earlier references to *Homestar Runner* Road Trip costumes). It can be hard, when looking at an item on the List that makes no sense to you, to figure out whether it's a reference to a piece of culture that you're just not familiar with or whether it's a reference to nothing at all.

I struggle with this because there are some canonical works that are simply missing from my own cultural education. One of them is the TV show *The Simpsons*. I know the names of the members of the nuclear family and that's about it. I'm sorry if this seems sacrilegious to you. I've definitely gotten that criticism before. But for what it's worth, I do carry around a lot of knowledge about *The Babysitters Club* and *10 Things I Hate About You*, so it's not like I bring nothing to the table.

Anyway, here are some *Simpsons* items. None of them mean anything to me as cultural touchstones, but a lot of them (like a clown bed) were extremely enjoyable to complete and to judge, even without any context.

10 ITEMS THAT REFERRED TO *THE SIMPSONS* AND ONE THAT DIDN'T

1993.175: What is the street address of the Simpsons? [2 points] and **1993.207:** What is Grandpa Simpson's first name? [1 point]

> The first *Simpsons* references on the list, and a good example of the kind of esoteric trivia items that appeared more often in a pre-Google age. The answers are "742 Evergreen Terrace" and "Abraham," respectively.

1996.291: The theme song from *The Simpsons* played on a balalaika. [30 points]

1997.023: Prank call The Pub using names from *The Simpsons* on Saturday night between 9 pm and 12 midnight; Judge will be there to accept calls and get team names. [3 points]

1997.192: A team member to have copious amounts of chewing gum removed from their hair via *The Simpsons* method, up until and including the Groundskeeper Willie way. [40 points]

> A reference to the episode "22 Short Films About Springfield" (3F18). After Lisa gets gum stuck in her hair, various characters offer suggestions as to how to remove it, including peanut butter, mayonnaise, olive oil, lemon juice, tartar sauce, chocolate syrup,

gravy, bacon fat, hummus, baba ganoush, and grape-
fruit juice. Groundskeeper Willie's suggestion was
that "chewin' gum's got ta be CHEWED out."

2000.122: Have I. Ron Butterfly's "In the Garden of Eden" played
on the organ at Bond Chapel. [40 points. 40 bonus points for
a contemporaneous service of either "Christian, Jewish, or
Miscellaneous" services]

> A reference to the episode "Bart Sells His Soul"
> (3F02), where Bart tricks the church organist into
> playing Iron Butterfly's "In-A-Gadda-Da-Vida."

2001.184: Working models of all of Homer Simpson's inventions. [41
points per invention]

> Refers to "The Wizard of Evergreen Terrace" (5F21),
> in which Homer invents an "EVERYTHING'S ALL
> RIGHT" alarm, a full-facial make-up gun, and a com-
> bination recliner/toilet.

2007.153: I know how much you like clowns, so I built you this bed.
Now you can laugh yourself to sleep! [70 points]

> From "Lisa's First Word" (9F08), a reference to
> Homer's terrifying attempts at creating a new bed
> for Bart. Team captains were almost universal
> in their dislike of the item (as its mere presence
> made team HQs, quote, "hella creepy"), causing the
> Judges to unanimously pass a sequel (2008.118: I
> know how much you like clowns, so I made you
> this canoe. Now you can laugh yourself to camp! [70
> points]) out of spite.

2010.82: Alright, nerds, time to get your trivia on. It's a Simpsons,
Star Wars, and firefly trivia contest! Send up to two trivia experts

to the Reynolds Club South Lounge on Thursday at 3 pm, and we'll see whose brains are properly geeked. [Δ points]

> This contest asked questions about O. J. Simpson, the Star Wars Missile Defense System, and fireflies, the insect. Participants did not find it as funny as the Judges did.

2014a.68: An elected public official who asserts, either on video or in person, that our country should move forward, not backward; upward, not forward; and always twirling, twirling, twirling towards freedom! [8 points, 2 additional points if the same official supports a policy of abortions for some, miniature American flags for others]

> From "Tree House of Horror VII" (4F02). Completed by Senator Kamala Harris for Snell-Hitchcock.

2015.81: A team member dragging the Stone of Shame into Judgment. [7 points. You are expected to drag the Stone of Triumph into your headquarters if your team wins the Hunt or said victory will be declared null and void]

> From "Homer the Great" (2F09). Notable for Snell-Hitchcock getting a legitimate 500-pound boulder for their stone.

SOMETIMES BEING A JUDGE SEEMS LIKE IT'S AS GOOD
as life gets. You get to ask for pretty much anything (within reason, or at least within the bounds of the law) and Scavvies will do
their best to give it to you. I've asked for items that I never got
(e.g., 2009.176, "Monozygotic human triplets at Judgment"—come
on, guys, I am *still waiting*), but Scav has made many of my dreams
come true. (For example, in 2006, I got an inspirational movie montage about studying for finals *and* a pair of glasses that turned
everything upside down! How cool is that?!)

But being a Judge isn't always such a dream come true. It
comes with conflict, anxiety, pressure, responsibility, and a lot of
tough decisions. Not everyone wants the role—and even if you do,
there are unavoidably going to be times when you regret it. All the
Judges can do is hope that cool items, excited Scavvies, and the
sense that they're a key part of something important make all the
sacrifices and the stress feel worth it.

ITEM 23:

RELITE NITELINE

Matthew Kellard

2002 SCAV HUNT

The unofficial motto of the University of Chicago is "Where fun comes to die," and, except during the Four Days, that's pretty accurate. Seasonal Affective Disorder is no joke, especially when the "season" in question lasts from October through April, and one's mental health can be pummeled under the pressure of the U of C's outrageous academic expectations.

Enter Niteline. In 1979, the administration created Niteline as a confidential, late-night crisis intervention phone service. It became more than that though, as the all-student Niteline volunteers took on the role of responding to any inquiry, whether by offering information, referring callers to professional help, or just being a general ear to cry into. I personally never made use of its services, but I liked the idea that Niteline was out there from 5:00 p.m. to 6:00 a.m. every night and that, if needed, I could call for any reason without fear of judgment.

Then, two months before Scav Hunt 2002 began, Niteline was permanently shuttered.

Around the same time, I had taken over as Head Judge of the Scavenger Hunt. Being a Judge was never something I had my heart set on. I mean, of course I had given it my all for the Shoreland team when it came to convincing my mom to FedEx me my Garbage Pail Kids collection, or constructing a 100-foot-tall Cookie Monster out of fabric and chicken wire on the main quad, or arranging four-part harmonies to be sung by myself and some other dudes wearing only straw boater hats. But it was mostly a weekend-long, drunken lark in my first year at college. When the friends who roped me onto our dorm's team subsequently roped me into applying to be a Judge, I just went along. I approached judging Scav Hunt like I'd approached competing in it: half-assedly and boozed into oblivion.

But by the following year, I had stumbled into the position of Head Judge, and I now had a strict sobriety policy to go along with binders full of notes, schedules, and various Scav Hunt arcana. I was spending exponentially more time orchestrating Scav Hunt than any other individual and nearly flunking myself out of financial aid in the process.

It was on my watch that the word came down of Niteline's cancellation. So in the best tradition of Scav Hunt, the Judges sought to rectify an injustice while simultaneously causing widespread irritation.

23. Relite Niteline. Each team must provide us with a phone number by the Captains' Summit. Judges must be able to call this phone number at any time between 17h00 and 06h00 throughout the Hunt. Phone must be answered in a minimum 2 rings with "Hello, Niteline!" Answerer must be prepared to resolve absolutely any problem the caller might have, and boy do we have problems. Remember to advertise your service to the public. [170 points]

Thursday night, in an age before search engines answered everything, the Judges tested out the lines with inconsequential requests.

What's the fastest way to get from Hutch Commons to Hot Doug's?

What happened last night on that new show The Bachelor?

What's that song that goes "nah na-na-na-nah na-na-na-nah na-na-nah na-na-nah na-na-na-nah"?

Which weapon beats Boomer Kuwanger in Mega Man X?

What the fuck is a Kuwanger?

This morphed into calls where we yelled lines from *Glengarry Glen Ross* into the phone ("You just cost me six thousand dollars! What are you going to do about it, asshole?!"), and in the end we kind of looked around and realized maybe this whole thing seemed more interesting on paper than it would end up being.

But then I called the Pierce team's Niteline, and my call lasted for an hour.

You see, being Head Judge was more responsibility and pressure than I had ever taken on in my life. As you may have gathered by now, putting together the Hunt is an immense production. At any given time, you could find me simultaneously chairing an hours-long Judges' meeting, planning competitive buzkashi (the polo-esque national sport of Afghanistan except with a dead calf instead of a ball) on tricycles in an ice rink, convincing the pathologically scared administration that students replacing the soda in the Bartlett vending machines with Schlitz or the existence of the "bulletproof athletic cup, and prove it" item would be no big deal, as well as applying for ever more funding for the whole "very serious" and "absolutely-essential-to-the-culture-of-the-university" shebang. And that's just a small sliver of the job. It's a lot. So, when I called Pierce's number and a Scavvie named Eleanor answered with "Hello, Niteline!" it all just came pouring out of me.

I told this stranger something like the following: "Um, hello. I think I'm having a panic attack. The administration is breathing down my neck about the quad party item and implying that Scav Hunt will be canceled if alcohol is present.

Of course, there's already no stopping *that* train, and anyway how am I supposed to ensure the survival of this event that thousands of people consider the most important tradition at this school while *also* being expected to produce a bigger and more spectacular Scav Hunt than any that's come before? Oh also, one Road Trip team accidentally committed a federal crime by taking a photo on government property because who knew, and they, like, *might* be in jail? Oh and! There's another rumor circulating about team A sabotaging team B's headquarters, so I might have to disqualify team A, who is arguably winning Scav Hunt right now. I think two Judges are fucking, and two others hate each other, maybe or maybe not related to the aforementioned fucking. Also, I just broke up with Jenny a couple of days ago. We were dating for two and a half years. Worst of all, I just noticed a GODDAMN TYPO ON PAGE ELEVEN OF THE LIST! What should I do?"

From Eleanor I got a far more receptive and understanding response than I had any right to. There is always an uneven Judge-Scavvie power dynamic, but this was more complex than the usual "feed us" and "entertain us" items. Eleanor listened, she asked questions, and she framed my crises in a new light. I talked about my relationship issues, my fear of making the wrong choices, and other deep psychological insecurities. It was a lunatic amount of vulnerability I was laying at a stranger's feet under the circumstances, but the craziest part was that it *worked*. Talking it through made me feel better, and it allowed me to handle the stress. Suddenly Scav Hunt Niteline wasn't just an item anymore. It was the real thing.

My calls got more frequent. The next day saw the previous crises get resolved, while new ones emerged. The party went fine, with an acceptable level of nudity, stunt-related injuries, and close calls with alcohol poisoning. But then, during cleanup, a bunch of Judges started kissing one another, until another group of Judges radioed to say that a fight was starting on 57th Street. A pack of frat dudes who didn't even go to the U of C had laid hands on one of the smaller female Judges, and from there punches were thrown. One of the Judges got his front tooth broken in half in the process. Also, my ex-girlfriend, Jenny, showed up to the math trivia/ *Dance Dance Revolution*/slap-bass-athon event with another guy, and I momentarily lost my vision from the anxiety.

Again Eleanor was patient and understanding, while the other Judges wondered what the hell I was doing crouching in some bushes with a phone hugged to my ear. That's not how a Head Judge is supposed to handle the Hunt. But I needed it. I called Eleanor ten times a day, just to talk, and that got me through to the end of Judgment Day. I did not end up in a psychiatric ward. Hell, I didn't even throw up. And that's thanks to Niteline.

I'd like to say that Eleanor and I ended up dating, or even that we stayed friends. It would be a much better end to the story. But that was not to be. My breakup was short-lived; Jenny and I got back together that summer and five years later were married. Eleanor and I kept in touch for a little while (she had slipped me her real phone number at the close of Judgment Day), but she graduated, and we quickly fell out of communication with each other. Some people who meet in the context of the Scavenger Hunt go on to form connections that last for decades. Other relationships only make sense within the bizarre, spectacular chaos of the Hunt itself. This turned out to be the latter.

I don't know what, if anything, the Niteline item meant to the Scavvies who completed it. For many of them, it was probably just one more thing that they had to do. And I don't know how Eleanor felt about playing the role of always-available one-way sounding board for the Head Judge, the guy who should have had it all under control. All I know is that somehow I didn't even know what I needed until the List gave it to me. That's just what Scav Hunt is like.

◇◇

Matt "MK" Kellard played for the Shoreland team as a first year in 2000 and joined the Judgeship in 2001, remaining active through 2005. He was Head Judge in 2002 and 2003 and Keeper of the Scrolls (responsible for the wording and presentation of the final List) in 2004. Matt lives in Los Angeles, California, working as a screenwriter for film and television. He credits Scav Hunt Judge meetings as his first experience working in a comedy writers room.

MATTHEW KELLARD'S ESSAY HINTS AT SCAV'S ROMAN-
tic side, but there are times when Scav has gotten much more hot and heavy than extended phone calls with a girl you don't know. For example, I think of this moment from the 2012 Scav Olympics: "WWII homecoming kiss marathon. Last couple standing with lips locked and both bodies at 45 degrees wins!"

You might consider that famous black-and-white photo of a Navy sailor locking lips with a woman on V-J Day in Times Square to be sweet, and you might imagine re-creating it with your own significant other to be fun, but you would be underestimating Scavvies' competitiveness. Our kiss-off was closer to a massacre than to a love fest. A few couples remained in kisses for upward of ten minutes while their teammates cheered them on. After the first ninety seconds, they were in obvious misery. Girls' backs arched them lower and lower until they were practically folded in half. Guys' arms trembled vigorously as they strove to continue to support their partners' weight. Chapped lips stayed pressed together, unmoving, growing drier and drier, while the kissers tried to breathe out of their noses. There was no reprieve except quitting, and Scavvies hate quitting.

Anyway, win or lose, the one thing all those couples had in common after the event ended was that, no matter how in love they were, none of them wanted to kiss again any time soon.

Of course, some Scav romances can last for a very long time, which makes sense: if you both agree on the significance of Scav Hunt, then you already share a lot of the important stuff in common.

ITEMS 282-83:
DO THAT

Nora Friedman
2005 SCAV HUNT

The great thing about Scav Hunt is that it forces you to do crazy, sometimes life-changing things to fulfill items that are difficult to explain to people who have not participated in the Hunt. The terrible thing about Scav Hunt is that it forces you to do crazy, sometimes life-changing things to fulfill items that are difficult to explain, and then you have to go and explain them to your *mom*.

This is a story of one of those items.

In the spring of 2005, I had been dating my boyfriend, Colin McFaul, for about a year. We'd been drawn together by our willingness to participate in a vegan date auction (despite the fact that neither of us is vegan) and by our mutual love for Scav Hunt and the hit nineties Nickelodeon series *Pete and Pete*. We were extremely compatible, and as we approached the end of our senior year we were already discussing our future together. At the same time, we were both deep into Scav Hunt planning: Colin had applied to be and been chosen as a Judge, while I was finally going to be a captain of the Burton-Judson team.

Of course, Judges are forbidden from revealing any plans for the upcoming hunt, and Colin stuck to that rule religiously: as close as we were, I knew nothing about what items he'd passed, or what happened at the hours-long Judges' meetings that he'd been attending all winter and spring. But when we got the List, in the early hours of May 6, 2005, I could tell immediately that Colin had written the last two items on it:

282. Do Anything for Love. Run right into Hell and back. Never forget the way I feel right now. Some days it don't come easy. Some days it don't come hard. Some days it don't come at all. Some nights breathe fire. Some nights be carved in ice. Some nights be like nothing I've ever seen before or will again. Be there til the final act. Take a vow and seal a pact. Some days pray for silence. Some days pray for soul. Some days just pray to the God of Sex and Drugs and Rock N Roll. Some nights lose the feeling. Some nights lose control. Some nights lose it all when you watch me dance and the thunder rolls. Never stop dreaming of me. Raise me up. Help me down. Get me right out of this Godforsaken town. Make it all a little less cold. Hold me sacred. Hold me tight. Colorize my life. Make it all a little less cold. Make me some magic with your own two hands. Build me an emerald city with these grains of sand. Give me something I can take home. Cater to every fantasy I got. Hose me down with holy water if I get too hot. Take me places I've never known. Do anything for love, but don't do that. [1 point each]

283. Do that. [33 points]

These items were, quite obviously, composed of lyrics from the Meat Loaf song "I'd Do Anything for Love (But I Won't Do That)." Knowing Colin as well as I did, I could easily identify that this was how he had incorporated his love of rock operas into the List. After I finished laughing, I turned to everyone else in the lounge and said, "Colin is totally responsible for items 282 and 283. Anyone know what we want to do for them?" The meaning of these lyrics is notoriously vague; there's an entire section in the song's Wikipedia entry

on "Perceived ambiguity of 'that,'" and Meat Loaf himself is
quoted as saying that "What is 'that'?" is one of the questions
he's asked most frequently. So exactly what this item was
looking for—if anything—was up to debate.

Elena Schroeter piped up that she was planning on
making a "Meat Loaf's adventures at the University of Chicago" comic book, with each of the sentences of the items as
separate illustrated pages. "Awesome," I said. "I think Colin
will really like that, and it means I don't have to propose!"
There were scattered giggles at my joke, and then of course
everyone dove back into the chaos of Scav Hunt.

But the idea kept coming back to me over the course of
the hunt. Probably due to sleep deprivation, I found the idea
of someone proposing funnier and funnier as the days went
on. My internal monologue went something like this: "HA,
boy, I bet that would surprise Colin, he obviously wouldn't
expect anyone to propose for that item, HA HA HA!"

By Judgment Day I was, as usual, wiped. I had slept little,
done crazy things, and basically just wanted to get my team
through Judgment so I could eat, shower, and sleep.

Connor Coyne, who is a good friend of ours, was judging the last page on the List. As we made it to the bottom
of that page, Elena proudly showed off the comic book. We
shared a few giggles as Elena displayed some of the more
amusing panels, including Meat Loaf miserably participating
in Kuviasungnerk/Kangeiko with the quote "Make it all a
little less cold."

As Connor was making notations on our Judgment sheet,
I leaned over and asked him, "Did we get full points for those
items?"

"Oh yeah," he said. "Looks good."

"Phew!" I said. "Because if we hadn't gotten full points, I
was going to propose to Colin!"

I assumed Connor would respond to this the same way

that my teammates had when I made this comment on the night of List Release, or roughly along the lines of my mental monologue. He did not. He stopped writing, looked me straight in the eye, and said, "I want to see that item."

Connor spun on his heel and started calling across the first floor of Ida Noyes for Colin. I assume at this point all the blood drained from my face and I looked like someone was trying to kill me. I whipped around and found the eyes of my sympathetic, amazing cocaptains Mira Kim (né Marq Hwang) and Brett Westphal, who were absolutely gobsmacked. I began to flail my hands and hyperventilate. "Ohmygodohmygodohmygod guys, guys, what did I just get myself into?"

I could still hear Connor calling for "Judge Colin to help judge an item" as I continued to spit out a series of nonsense words. Mira and Brett were trying to reassure me, saying things like "You don't have to do anything you don't want to" and other supportive comments. Word was starting to spread around the room that something was going on for BJ's item 283, and the judging of all other items stopped as everyone waited for Colin to arrive.

My adrenaline levels were running sky-high, and I had one of those moments of rare clarity born of a crisis situation: I loved Colin, and I knew he loved me. We had already discussed how we would arrange our plans for the next few years to remain together, regardless of where we ended up due to graduate school. We were good for each other. We understood each other and shared similar values. There was no reason *not* to get engaged.

Colin had finally been located and Connor was bringing him back into the room. I turned to Mira and Brett and said something like, "It's cool, guys, I got this."

"Wait," said Brett, "you are actually going to do this?"

"Yeah," I said. "Yeah, I am."

I turned around to catch Colin's eye as he confusedly

looked around. Taking a deep breath, I stepped forward to intercept him in the middle of the room. Then I got down on one knee, took his hand, and proceeded to disjointedly ask Colin to marry me.

I can't remember much of what I said, but I do remember that I told him that the reason I was doing this was because "I know you wrote this item, you son of a bitch." I also remember that once I finished my rant, Colin leaned down and pulled me up into a hug. "Do you mean it?" he asked.

"Yes, I do," I said.

He smiled at me and hugged me again and said, "Yes."

Scavvies cheered. Photos were taken. Later that evening, when the team standings were released, members from the FIST brought us champagne. My team came in last place, which was great because I was already wearing my hand-made BJ "LAST PLACE, MOST FUN" T-shirt.

Only one thing remained to do: tell my mother. So, a few days after Judgment, I called home. "Hey, Mom," I said, "happy belated Mother's Day!"

"Oh, thanks, honey. How was the scavenger hunt?" she replied.

"It was good, lots of fun. Also, uh, for an item, I kind of asked Colin to marry me."

My mother sounded confused when she asked, "In the scavenger hunt, or in real life?"

"Um, both?" I meekly responded.

A loooong pause. Then, with the sigh that everyone gets from their moms when they participate in something that truly confounds them: "Now, why did you go and do a thing like that?"

I exhaled and said, "Well, Mom, how much do you know about the singer Meat Loaf?"

Epilogue: My mother quickly got over her shock, and she, my father, and my sisters happily brought Colin into our family fold. Two years later, Colin and I were married in Rockefeller Chapel, with many of our Scav friends in attendance. Our first dance at the wedding was, appropriately, "I'd Do Anything for Love (But I Won't Do That)." We've been together ever since.

<><><><><><><><><><><><><><><><><><><><><><><><><><><><><><><><><><><><><><><><><><><><><><><><><>

Nora Friedman graduated in 2005 with a degree in the history, philosophy, and social studies of science and medicine. She Scavved from 2001 to 2006 for Burton-Judson and was team captain in 2005 and 2006. She and Colin left Chicago for New Orleans shortly after their wedding to attend graduate school at Tulane University. Nora got her masters in parasitology in 2009 and her PhD in epidemiology in 2013 (dual focus in infectious disease and reproductive epidemiology) from Tulane University School of Public Health and Tropical Medicine. She worked at the CDC in Atlanta from 2014 to 2017 at the National Center for HIV/AIDS, Viral Hepatitis, STD, and TB Prevention. She now works at the Chicago Center for HIV Elimination in the Department of Medicine at the University of Chicago.

WHAT'S THE ONLY THING THAT COULD BE AS ROMANTIC as a Scav engagement? Why, a Scav wedding, of course!

ITEM 0:

SERIOUSLY, THIS IS A REAL WEDDING

Christian Kammerer

2015 SCAV HUNT

On New Year's Day 2014, on Europe's holiest ground (Vienna Central Cemetery, at the grave site of Falco, renowned singer of "Rock Me Amadeus"), I went down on one knee and asked my girlfriend of nine years to marry me. She said yes. But as anyone who's tried to plan a wedding could tell you, the hard part was just beginning.

Nine months later, we'd become accustomed to the nebulous intermediary state of "being engaged" but had made zero progress in actually planning the wedding. A variety of factors conspired against it. For one thing, we lived in Germany, but the vast majority of our family and friends resided back in the United States. Asking everyone to fly overseas for the wedding would be cost-prohibitive. My fiancée is no fan of formal ceremonies under any circumstances and would, if it were all the same, prefer to elope. At the same time, we were the first of the grandchildren in our respective extended families to get engaged, and elderly Catholic relatives were insisting upon tradition.

While puzzling over this conundrum, I was *also* thinking about plans for Scav Hunt. Admittedly, that is my default state, because I *love* Scav Hunt. I was a Scavvie for all four years of undergrad and by 2015 had been a Judge for eleven.

During my undergraduate years, the big Friday night Scav event was a party on the quads, a vast, sprawling affair that drew hundreds of attendees from the ranks of hard-core Scavvies and passersby alike. Indeed, it was the big party of the U of C school year. Tragically, the school administration put the kibosh on it following the legendary Cobb Party of 2006. Over the years, we'd tried to replace the party with less raucous Friday night events, but they just weren't the same, and they had become progressively less memorable and well attended.

At this point in Scav's history, we needed something new, something that had never been done before. Something to draw in the crowds, a spectacle, a celebration instead of just another item to tick off the List. Enter: Scav Wedding.

My fiancée needed minimal convincing, since she'd been a Scavvie herself. I said, "So I know you don't like weddings."

And she said, "That's right."

And I said, "But what if, and just hear me out on this, it was a Scav wedding."

And she agreed that this sounded like a wedding she could really get behind. (Which is, by the way, clear indication that she is what is known as "a keeper.")

So I set the Judges to work on creating our wedding. The Judges Emeriti were also informed of the event via email and instructed to "Kindly come up with items through which teams may increase the jollity of this Holiest of Scavraments. P.S. This is not a joke." We gave the Judges broad discretionary powers to shape the event, meaning there were aspects of the wedding unknown even to us until the List was released, about forty-four hours before we walked down the aisle.

While the Judges were cooking up wedding items, I was managing things on the "this is also a 100 percent real, legally binding wedding ceremony that our entire families will be attending" side: reserving hotel blocks, planning catering, calling in the accumulated favors of ten years attending the University of Chicago, all that stuff.

The invitations posed something of a problem, however. Obviously nobody outside the Judgeship could know that our wedding would be composed of Scav items. The Judges would lay down their lives before revealing any of the Hunt's mysteries before List Release. At the same time, for folks out of state or overseas to be able to attend this wedding, people needed to know that it was happening somewhat earlier than two days prior to its occurrence. But with many of our friends being current or former U of Cers, and several of them still active Scavvies, merely telling them the date of the wedding was guaranteed to raise suspicion.

To defuse this, we leaned into the obvious temporal concordance. We didn't wait for them to bring it up; we volunteered it. Of *course* we were getting married during Scav Hunt, we explained, because we know that is when the largest number of our friends will be in Hyde Park *anyway*. Given how many of our buddies come back for Scav Hunt, it just makes sense to do it then and save everyone a trip, right? Right.

With this stated out in the open, only one of my friends still asked, "Are you going to be serenaded by a chorus of undergrads as part of item 28, or whatever?" To this I could only reply, "What kind of madman would let Scav Hunt into his wedding?" (His response later, once the Hunt had started: "I should have known you were *exactly* that kind of madman!")

The ceremony would occur in that most stately of campus buildings, Rockefeller Chapel, a Gothic revival cathedral that houses the world's largest carillon. Picture Westminster Abbey, only filled with about a thousand people in duct tape and utility kilts who haven't slept since Tuesday.

One of the items associated with the event was to present a dramatic reading of a passage dealing with love in one of the great sci-fi or fantasy novels or films; in the hours before the ceremony, while our guests were enjoying barbecue, the Judges were rehearsing the hell out of the Scavvies to make sure it all went right. (By contrast, those of us who were actually in the wedding party did no rehearsal whatsoever.)

SW8. And now, a reading from the Gospel of Nerd. In the style of children acting out the nativity story of Luke 2:1-20, each team will prepare a moving, two-minute-tops reading from a passage dealing with love in one of the great sci-fi or fantasy novels or films. Concurrent with the reading, appropriately costumed Scavvies from your team give a dramatic rendering of the action upon the altar. [15 points]

These efforts paid off. People claim your wedding is one of the happiest days of your life, and it turns out that's even more true when you get to walk down the aisle in a re-creation of the climactic scene of *The Muppets Take Manhattan*, complete with a smoke machine.

SW9. Please note that the Scavvenwedding will commence in the style of 1984's *The Muppets Take Manhattan*. Send your team's choral penguin to Rockefeller Chapel at 5:00 p.m. on Friday for rehearsal, having memorized the gooey Muppets dreamhymn: "He'll Make Me Happy." [6 points]

Throughout the ceremony, gags from Scav history were embraced and given deeper meaning. The officiant (a dear friend and Judge Emeritus himself) dressed as a sea captain, referring in part to a 2007 Road Trip item whose origin is too byzantine to detail here. (Item 248, if you're curious.) A litany of *Simpsons* references were indulged in: bride and groom pig cuff links were gifted, time travel advice was given, "special rings" were exchanged, and the entirety of I. Ron Butterfly's "In the Garden of Eden" was played on the organ with vocal accompaniment from the collected attendees.

The Scavvies' dramatic readings proved extremely moving. Criswell's opening narration from *Plan 9 from Outer Space* was recited not once but twice (*mostly* coincidentally). One team performed the wedding scene from *The Princess Bride*, as we were, after all, engaging in the sacred act of "mawwiage." People in the audience legitimately cried when a quartet of sleep-deprived college students performed a moving scene from *Babylon 5* (a television program that neither my fiancée nor I had ever even seen). And in the end, we "recessed" by being crowd-surfed down the aisle and pelted with coleslaw before driving off in a car pursued by tin can velociraptors.

SW1. Muldoon claimed that raptors could move "50, 60 miles per hour" over open ground, but that's a tad generous from what we know of theropod biomechanics. You know how they could go that fast, though? If they were being dragged behind a moving car! Construct a small Velociraptor made of tin cans, to pursue the "Just Married"-mobile. [4 points]

We finished off the night with nine wedding cakes, each one homemade by a different team and shaped to resemble something my fiancée and I loved: crustaceans, Godzilla, the forest moon of Endor, Pokémon, *Goosebumps*, the Eurovision Song Contest, Scrat from *Ice Age*, "a big pile of VHS tapes," and *Space Jam*.

Going into all this, some might have questioned the wisdom of involving an institution described as "a microcosm of chaos" in so major a life event as one's wedding. Some in the university community already consider Scav to be a gathering of weirdos to be avoided, and to them, a Scav wedding must have seemed like the height of lunacy.

For us, though, that "gathering of weirdos" meant creativity and community. In a celebration of commitment, who better to include than the people you know would drop everything and board an airplane not knowing their destination, would alter the surface of the moon, would build a nuclear reactor? There may have been a tinge of madness to the proceedings, certainly. But for us, it was perfect.

◇◇

Christian Kammerer (AB '03—biological sciences and geophysical sciences, MS '06—biological sciences, PhD '09—biological sciences) Scavved for the Snell-Hitchcock team from 2000 to 2003 and has served as a Scav Hunt Judge since 2003. He is currently research curator of paleontology at the North Carolina Museum of Natural Sciences, specializing in mammal origins and mass extinctions. He slept in the Pierce team's *Simpsons* clown bed (2007, item 153) from 2007 to 2012.

19 ITEMS DEDICATED TO UNIVERSITY OF CHICAGO FACULTY, LORE, AND CAMPUS LIFE

1990.170: A U of C Professor to sing "Wild Thing." [50 points]

> Completed by Ted Cook, the dean of students at the time.

1992.31: A professor with ID to act out a skit from "Wayne's World" complete with the terms "SCHWING" and "NOT" and the appropriate physical motions while wearing the Wayne's World hat. [45 points]

> Completed by David Bevington, Phyllis Fay Horton Distinguished Service Professor Emeritus in the Humanities. Once described by Harold Bloom as "one of the most learned and devoted of Shakespeareans." And, as this item proved, a hell of a SCHWINGer.

1993.152: A copy of a letter by an alum sent to the U of C saying they won't contribute any more due to the cancellation of Sleep Out. Note: they must have contributed in the past. [10 points]

> While Scav is now the most notable Mother's Day tradition, this was not always the case. Mother's Day at the University of Chicago was once known for the Sleep Out, a tradition in which students would camp out on the quads overnight so as to be first in line to register for fall classes. A new computerized

course registration system rendered the Sleep Out unnecessary, which gave alumni one more reason to say that "this place isn't what it used to be," a complaint that has been made basically every year before or since then.

1994.135: A U of C Professor yelling "yahoo!" repeatedly for as long as it takes to judge the page [25 points]

> Energetically completed by Guy Alitto, Associate Professor in History and East Asian Languages and Civilizations. We understand that he was forgiven for throwing some "Yippee!"s into the mix as well.

1994.242: A complete copy of the article where the U of C social life was listed as #300 [14 points]

> This could be found in the issue of *Inside Edge* college magazine released in November 1993, which ranked the U of C lower than such party schools as Oral Roberts University (293), Brigham Young University (295), and the United States Military Academy (299).

1995.149: A Business School student stealing a "Romper Room" cushion from a U of C undergraduate [23 points]

> The "Romper Room" was the affectionate nickname of the former North Reading Room in Harper. It was a big padded affair, set up as a lounge and covered in orange pillows, beloved by all the undergrads who studied there. Around 1995 the Romper Room was destroyed and replaced with conference rooms for Graduate School of Business students, earning the endless enmity of the undergraduate student body.

1996.156: A University official to tell us the story of Professor Throckmorton. [32 points]

> According to campus legend, Professor Throckmorton was a U of C professor who went insane and spent the rest of his days as a scraggly-bearded hobo, busking for change in the wilds of Hyde Park.

1997.222: The U of C admissions booklet—"Nightmares and Hegemonies: The Real Story." Take "Dreams and Choices" and highlight every obfuscation, misrepresentation, and blatant falsehood. Bonus points for correctly identifying whatever it is that the lovely Jessica Doyle is sculpting out of snow. [20 points, 6 point bonus]

> "Dreams and Choices" was the lofty title of the college admissions booklet at the time.

1997.223: A list of 101 ransom demands the Hannabomber should have made to the University [10 points]

> Hanna Holborn Gray was the tenth University of Chicago president, serving in the office from 1978 to 1993; the first female (full) president of a major university in the United States; and, most importantly, the figure who oversaw the creation of Scav Hunt. Of particular note is her university portrait. Beyond the mere fact that it came out a little kitsch, the portrait was stolen twice from its location in Hutch Commons, the second time by the so-called "Hannabomber," who took the time to send taunting photographs and manifestos to student paper the *Maroon*.

1998.308: Complete the analogy: Football:Education::Bullfighting:____. [3 points]

"College football is a sport that bears the same re-
lation to education that bullfighting does to agri-
culture." Then-university president Robert Maynard
Hutchins would swipe this Elbert Hubbard quotation
in justifying why the University of Chicago ditched
football in 1939.

1999.314: Though Ted O'Neill has remarkably good looks, let's be frank:
He can't dress at all. He should casually admit that he had never before
had fashion sense, and he should then thank God for your team's
eagerness to take him to Barney's and outfit him right. [569 points.
Your team is immediately disqualified if a tie featuring Princeton's
colors appears]

Ted O'Neill, known to Judges and Scavvies alike
as the "Dean of Love," was the charming dean of
admissions at the University of Chicago for twenty
years. A friend of Scav, he went so far as to act as a
celebrity guest Judge in 1996.

2000.24: Prove that a U of C diploma has the absorbing power of
Brawny Brand paper towels. [75 points]

2005.213: A photomosaic of the Reg, made up of at least 100 photos
of happy U of C students. [23 points]

2006.124: Who wears short shorts? Why, tenured faculty members,
of course! [10 points]

David Bevington, again.

2008.149: How many housing rules can you break in one moment? We
don't care. How many can your RA break, that we care about. Your
RH? Your AD? Sherry Gutman? Points per rule violation. [$R \times I$ points,
where R =number of rule violations and I = 1 point for an RA, 2 points

for an RH, 5 points for an AD, 10 points for Katie Callow Wright and 20 for Sherry Gutman. Note that if we've seen Sherry Gutman smoking a joint on a fire escape we don't care about anything Jim Wessel does so only bring us rule violations by one person.]

> RA is Resident Advisor, RH is Resident Head, Sherry Gutman was the dean for housing and dining services, and Katie Callow-Wright was the associate dean and director of undergraduate student housing.

2009.252: An authentic University of Chicago diploma, to be stamped with [REDACTED] in huge letters at Judgment. [3 points]

2014a.100: Accompany a campus tour group! Every time the tour guide talks, play the saddest backing song you can on a single violin. [7 points]

2014b.61: Publicly, Dean Boyer's preferred mode of exercise may be bicycling, but deep down we think he may have another passion. Convince him or another dean to lead members of your team on a Prancercise tour of the Quads. [9 points for an assistant dean. 11 for a full dean. 14 for the man himself]

> Completed by John Boyer, Dean of the College and the Martin A. Ryerson Distinguished Service Professor of History, author of *The University of Chicago: A History*, and, as it turns out, a darn good Prancerciser.

2017.222: By Friday at 9:30 a.m., place somewhere on the Main Quad a life-sized cutout of Dean Nondorf which shouts "helpful" admissions advice at passersby. [14 points]

> James G. Nondorf is the current dean of admissions at the University of Chicago.

ITEM 58:

SHORETRISLAND

Leila Sales
2003 SCAV HUNT

As you can tell by now, having nearly reached the end of this anthology, I am devoted to Scav Hunt and I have been since my very first Scav, in 2003, playing for the Shoreland team. What might come as more of a surprise is that I am pretty useless as a Scavvie. I do not know how to cook or code or construct. I can't sew or play music or drive long distances or solve puzzles or eat anything disgusting without throwing up. I was so excited for my first Scav Hunt, but I remember growing increasingly frustrated and despondent at the List Reading. Not only was I not useful for most of the items, but many of them I didn't even *understand*. Like, every time-specific event was written in "French Revolutionary time," but nowhere did it *say* it was in French Revolutionary time; you just had to figure that out. I recall numerous references to "AND1," something which I did not then and do not to this day know anything about.

There was nothing about item 58 that obviously played to my strengths, not least because I suspected I didn't ac-tually *have* any strengths when it came to Scav. But at least I understood the impossible thing that it was asking for.

58. We want to play SearsTris Tower (or, alternatively, HanTrisCock). Make Alexei Pajitnov proud. [222 points. 25 bonus points if it is set to appropriate music]

Our captains discussed. To play *Tetris* using the windows of one of the major downtown office buildings would require an elaborate computer hack (definitely not something I was going to bring to the table, as "proficient in Microsoft Office Suite" is the top level of technical bragging I do on my résumé), or it would have cost about $30,000 (which is also not a skill set that I have hanging around). This item could not be done, Captain Josh concluded, and we should give up on securing the Sears Tower and focus our energies where they would actually pay off.

"But it doesn't have to be on the Sears Tower, does it?" I suggested on Saturday afternoon. "We could play *Tetris* on any tall building with a lot of windows. We could do it . . . here."

"That's not what the item is asking for," Josh responded, but even as he said it, I could tell he was thinking it over. The Shoreland was a fourteen-story residence hall housing around 650 undergraduates. Unlike the other dorms, which were built specifically for university students, the Shoreland had once been a big apartment building facing toward Lake Michigan. And this meant that we had an asset available to no other team: lots and lots of windows in a grid formation.

"All right," Josh said. "ShoreTrisLand. Let's do it." He told the Judges to come at 10 p.m., ready to play *Tetris*, and he told me to rally the troops.

We quickly realized that we couldn't get every dorm room to volunteer their windows for our *Tetris* game. Out of the 650 residents, maybe fifty of them considered themselves part of the Shoreland Scav team, which meant a lot of people would want nothing to do with this. Fortunately, every floor's lounge, located in the middle of the building, had seven front-facing windows. So we decided that the seven lounge windows on nine consecutive floors would form our playing grid.

I got to work. I went through every lounge on every floor, masking tape in hand, and taped labels to each of the windows: "5A" for the first window on the fifth floor, "6G" for the last window on the sixth floor, and on and on and on. Meanwhile, in the lobby, my friend Becca painted dozens of giant signs, one corresponding to each labeled window.

On my way through the building, I knocked on the door of every single dorm room. If the residents were home, I told them to come to their floor's lounge at ten o'clock. If they weren't, I left notes under their doors.

The Judges later told me that they had intended for teams to design computer programs to flick lights on and off. But we didn't have a computer program. All we had was 650 residents. And in Scav Hunt, well, you use what you've got.

As 10 p.m. approached, a dozen of us stood outside, Becca's painted signs at the ready. We had laid them out in piles—all the fifth-floor signs in one place, all the sixth-floor signs in another, and so on. The plan was that one Scavvie outside would be in charge of each floor and would raise the signs to tell the Scavvies inside the lounges which window shades to open and close.

The only problem was, there weren't any Scavvies inside.

We stared up at the Shoreland, all its lounge lights on, all its window shades open. We needed about seventy participants to pull this off—nine of us outside to raise the signs and sixty-three more inside, one to man each window shade. We could do it with less, maybe, but not much less. And even if we had seventy dedicated Scavvies on our team—which we didn't—some of them were by necessity working on other items or had been called to other events. We needed help from the normal people, the people who were just hanging out in their dorm rooms and doing reading or getting ready to go out to parties, the people who didn't care that it was Scav Hunt.

In typical Chicago fashion, a fierce wind was blowing, and large raindrops had begun to fall. One of our cell phones rang. "There's going to be a thunderstorm," said the Scavvie who was calling.

"Fine," we said.

"The weatherman says there's a tornado watch."

"Fine," we said.

"Should you come inside?"

"No," we said.

The Judges showed up then. All of them. Usually you get the Judge who wrote the item, maybe a couple others who want to see something cool. This was a dozen Judges, and they all wanted to play *Tetris* on the windows of a building.

As soon as the Judges arrived, the sky opened and the rain came crashing down, so loudly that we could barely hear Becca's boom box plinking out the *Tetris* theme song. Our paper signs instantly disintegrated into uselessness. The Judges huddled together under umbrellas, their eyes raised toward the Shoreland, ready to be amazed.

And there, silhouetted in every window on every floor, stood the Scavvies. They had come, after all, a hundred of them or more. Hands grasping the window shades, they awaited our commands—commands which, suddenly, thanks to the rain's destroying the signs, we could not give.

It kept pouring. The Judges looked at us, like, *Now what?* And the Scavvies on every floor looked down with the same expression.

Now what?

Now a new plan emerged. Nine of us outside called

nine Scavvies inside, one on each floor. I was the link to the twelfth floor. We would stay on the phone the whole time.

And then, Josh began to play *Tetris*. (Fortunately, he had spent much of his youth playing *Tetris*, so this came to him naturally—*Tetris* is yet another thing that I am useless at.)

"Lower the shade on 12F!" Josh shouted at me.

"12F!" I shouted into my phone.

"12F!" The Scavvie in charge of the twelfth floor shouted at the girl in the window of 12F.

And 12F went down.

A ripple of awe went through the Judges. We were doing this.

"11F!" Josh shouted, and the process began again.

Slowly, surely, a *Tetris* piece took shape. And slowly, surely, it moved down the board.

The Scavvies followed orders beautifully and blindly. Unable to see the game, knowing only what was happening on their own floor and at their own windows, they had no idea what pieces they were forming. Those of us soaking wet in the rain outside were the only ones who could see the playing board as a whole. We never stopped screaming into our phones. "I need 12A and B up! Right now! Up, up, raise them, now! KEEP 12C DOWN DON'T TOUCH 12C!"

When the board was half-filled, the Judges told us we could stop. "Clear everything!" we shrieked into our phones. "Every shade up!" Our indoor teammates scrambled to raise all the blinds simultaneously. And then, in windows B through E on floors 6 through 7, Scavvies held up signs.

"What does that say?" one Judge wondered. Then—"Oh! They spell GAME OVER!"

In the rain and the confusion, I had forgotten entirely about the "game over" signs that Becca had painted and we had left in those lounges, the only signs to escape the deluge.

None of us outside had given the command to lift those signs. But that's okay. Because our teammates didn't forget.

To this day, when asked in job interviews what I consider to be my greatest accomplishment, I answer: the time I organized a hundred people to play *Tetris* on the windows of a building. It was beautiful, it was legendary, and it made me realize that I'm *not* useless, after all. Sure, I can't cook or code or construct. I can't sculpt or catch anything that's thrown at me no matter how short the distance or speak multiple languages or recite more than the first two digits of pi.

But I can identify people who *can* do all of those things, and I can organize them into action. I can have a creative vision, and I can't really achieve it, but I can *facilitate* its achievement. I can make that vision sound like something that people want to be a part of. I can exhort those people to action, and I can give them the resources they need to make their final products as good as possible. That's the sort of Scavvie I am, that's the sort of person I am, and that is how I made this book. I hope you judge it worthy of receiving full points.

◇◇

Leila Sales grew up outside of Boston and graduated from the University of Chicago in 2006 with a degree in psychology. Since that time, she has been an editor at Penguin Random House and the author of six young adult novels, including *This Song Will Save Your Life* and *If You Don't Have Anything Nice to Say*. Learn more at leilasales.com, or follow her @LeilaSalesBooks.

ACKNOWLEDGMENTS

Like Scav Hunt itself, this book was truly a team effort. Just as you cannot build a working Strandbeest alone in only four days, so too could I not have edited this book without the collected talents of many friends and colleagues.

First and foremost, a huge thanks to the University of Chicago for supporting Scav Hunt in so many ways. Thank you for gathering all these crazy, creative intellects on one neo-Gothic campus and giving us an environment where we can play and explore to our full capabilities.

Thanks to Hot Side Hot for your cleverness, vision, tradition, and follow-through. Belonging to this community is one of the great honors of my life. Like so many good things in the world, this book exists thanks only to your ingenuity.

Special thanks to a couple members of the Judgeship for the crucial roles they played in creating this book, specifically Connor Coyne, who developed the concept alongside me from day one, and Patrick "Tricky" Augustine, keeper of Scav history and legacy, who compiled and annotated all of the lists in here.

To the Scavvies, who inspire me and show me what wonders are possible with a little tenacity and duct tape.

To my agent, Stephen Barbara (also a proud U of C alum!); his assistant, Claire Draper; my editor, Timothy Mennel; Tim's patient editorial associate, Rachel Kelly Unger; Lauren Salas; Caterina MacLean; and the rest of the team at the University of Chicago Press.

A huge thanks to the contributors and to all those who submitted essays—thank you for sharing your stories and for your willingness to work with me on revisions. A bonus thanks to those who provided photographs.

Thanks to my parents, who made it possible for me to attend and thrive at the University of Chicago in the first place.

And finally, thanks to the receptionist at the Henry Crown Field House who reluctantly gave me permission to borrow a ten-gallon cooler for Scav's 2003 Friday night party on the quads. I know I said I'd return it to you in the same condition in which you'd lent it to me, and I know that isn't exactly what happened, but I promise it was worth it.

APPENDIX A
A LIST OF SCAV HUNT TEAMS

The names, sizes, and formations of Scav Hunt teams are constantly evolving. An entire book could be written just chronicling the histories of the different teams. But that is, thankfully, not this book. For our purposes, here is just a partial list of teams mentioned over the preceding chapters.

For clarity, note that all first years and many older students live in dorms, and within each dorm there are multiple "houses." The adults in charge of each dorm are called the Resident Masters (or RMs), the adults in charge of each house are Resident Heads (RHs), and the upperclassmen in charge of each house are Resident Advisors (RAs).

BROOVER: A combination of "Breckinridge" (a dorm) and "Hoover" (a house within Max Palevsky). Active 2004-2008.

BURTON-JUDSON: A dorm, sometimes called "BJ." Active 1998-present.

CHAMBERLIN: A house in BJ that fielded its own team from 1987 to circa 1992.

THE FIST: An acronym for "the Federation of Independent Scav Teams," a team unaffiliated with any university housing. Known in its earliest incarnation as the Lush Puppies. Active 2002-2011.

GASH: An acronym for "Graduate and Alumni Scav Hunt Team," a team designed for and by alumni. Active 2008-present.

MACPIERCE: A combination of "Maclean" and "Pierce," two dorms that formed a single Scav team. Active 2006-2012.

THE MAROON: The student newspaper the *Chicago Maroon*, which fielded its own team for a few years in the nineties and early 2000s. Otherwise, the *Maroon* over the years has generally been anti-Scav, once describing Scav in its pages as "Allegedly, a fun-filled U of C tradition. Think of Nazi Germany without the Nazis or the Germans, but the same general esprit de corps."

MATHEWS: A house in BJ that fielded its own team from 1997 to 2000.

MAX PALEVSKY: A dorm. Sometimes referred to as "Max," "Palevsky," or "Max P." Active 2002–present.

SHORELAND: A dorm. Active 1997–2009.

SNITCHCOCK: A combination of "Snell" and "Hitchcock," two dorms that form a single Scav team. Active 1993–present.

SOUTH CAMPUS: A dorm team, sometimes referred to as "Scampi." Active 2010–present.

APPENDIX B
KEY LOCATIONS

COBB: The main undergraduate classroom building

EX LIBRIS CAFÉ: A café in the Regenstein Library

HARPER: A classroom building and library

HUTCH COMMONS: Short for "Hutchinson Commons," a large room in the Reynolds Club that serves as a dining hall and student lounge

HUTCH COURTYARD: The courtyard just outside of Hutch Commons, adjacent to the main quads

IDA NOYES: Also sometimes called simply "Ida," the building where Judgment occurs

THE PUB: The university's on-campus bar, located in the basement of Ida Noyes

THE QUADS: The university's main campus quadrangle

THE REGENSTEIN LIBRARY: The main library, also called "the Reg"

THE REYNOLDS CLUB: The university's primary student center, home to meeting rooms, event spaces, food facilities, and a number of student organizations

ROCKEFELLER CHAPEL: A neo-Gothic cathedral on the university's campus, built in 1928, home to the world's largest carillon, with seating for more than 1,500

THE SEMINARY CO-OP: One of the school's bookstores, also known as the "Sem Co-Op"